THE NECESSARY LEARNING

Liberal Arts and Sciences, Defense and Reform

Edited, with an Introduction by
Robert Moynihan

UNIVERSITY
PRESS OF
AMERICA

Lanham • New York • London

Copyright © 1989 by

University Press of America,® Inc.

4720 Boston Way
Lanham, MD 20706

3 Henrietta Street
London WC2E 8LU England

Printed in the United States of America

British Cataloging in Publication Information Available

70136392

Library of Congress Cataloging-in-Publication Data

The Necessary learning : liberal arts and sciences : defense and
reform / edited, with an introduction, by Robert Moynihan.
p. cm.
Papers presented at a colloquium on the liberal arts and sciences
at the State University of New York, Oneonta.
1. Universities and colleges—United States—Curricula—
Congresses. 2. Humanities—Study and teaching (Higher)—United
States—Congresses. 3. Science—Study and teaching (Higher)—United
States—Congresses. I. Moynihan, Robert, 1936–
    LB2361.5.N43   1988
378'.199'0973—dc 19   88–26185 CIP
ISBN 0–8191–7204–9 (alk. paper)

CONTENTS

This book is dedicated to my colleagues who helped plan the conference and who attended the meetings on the liberal arts and sciences on the Oneonta campus of the State University of New York; special thanks to Reuben James, Department of Physics, the members of the Philosophy Department, and to Fred Ermlich, expediter extraordinary.

I am grateful to Barbara Ackerly for her exemplary patience and skill in typing and processing this opus.

Introduction

According to callow myth, two kinds of colleges and universities exist in the United States. One, Belve U., a private institution, leads its students to the golden traditions of the past and to the capital rewards of the future, weaving a gilded network of tradition with monetary gain. The other, Sweat College, is a training camp for the lower and slower orders of technicians and clerks in the bureaucracy. They labor life-long with the frustrations of economic scarcity, ill-assorted ignorance, and the burdens of mid-class gray collar survival, without benefit of a parental cash-cushion or safety net. These two kinds of institution are as exclusive as rival sororities and fraternities. The members of Belve U. and Sweat have little or no contact, live in different urbs and sub-urbs, and pursue, with differing levels of income, totally separate life-styles.

As well, the two classes are educated differently. At Belve U., tweedy professors talk about Aristotle and great ideas. At Sweat, the talk is as factual as the Dickens' parody of the school room in the aptly named Hard Times, with its own demi-professor, Gradgrind, insisting on nothing but facts. At Sweat, the professors are wed to polyester in ill-matched colors, such as blue and brown, and an instructor often wears the same outfit and the same fixed idea all the year long. In their faculty lounges, Belve U-ers talk of great ideas and their latest publications. Sweats talk about poor student performance on multiple choice tests and what was on TV the night before.

The problem with this antithetical myth is simple: it's invalid. The exclusive heights of Belve

U. and the abysmal depths of Sweat are on a more equal level than either cares to admit.

For instance, changes in the "classical" rhetorical training took place in both the public and private institutions at about the same time. Latin as a requirement for the B.A. was dropped at Yale long before it passed from the American public school curriculum, and both private and public institutions of higher learning have debased their curricula with "History through Film," "Baseball Fiction," "Lyrics of Rock and Roll."

Moreover, the drive to "professionalism" was made by Yale, Harvard, and the University of Pennsylvania some while ago, their example followed by dozens of other prestigious campuses. Living in co-existence on those campuses are schools of business, medicine, dentistry, law, engineering, and departments of English, foreign languages, history, comparative literature, philosophy. It would be impolite and impolitic to ask, even at the pinnacle of American prestige and endowment, Harvard, which department wields the most political power within the campus, or which is the better funded, the School of Business or the Department of English? The same nearly ludicrous disproportion of power within that campus exists also at Yale and Penn. Yet, on all these campuses, the liberal pretension lives on, hallowed by myth, status, and yes, literate necessity.

The most striking recent comment on American higher education comes, nonetheless, from a non-Belve U. promontory. In a remarkably candid and mordant book on status in the United States, Paul Fussell admits and then celebrates the fact that socially exclusive classes inhabit the country. They don't coexist, but live in different enclaves--the greater the wealth, the more invisible the class: "Top-out-of-sight" Fussell calls its members. At one point in the book, however, Fussell, who labored some three decades as a professor and writer at Rutgers University, a state institution supported by

New Jersey rate payers, delivers these dicta in <u>Class</u>:
A Guide Through the American Status System:

> The assumption that a 'college degree' means
> something without the college's being
> specified . . . dies very hard. . . .
> A degree from Amherst or Williams or
> Harvard or Yale should never be confused
> with having one from Eastern Kentucky
> University or Hawaii Pacific College or
> Arkansas State or Bob Jones.

Of the proportional increase from the 1940's to the
1970's of the college population, thirteen percent to
forty-three percent, Fussell observes:

> But no, it was still about 13 percent, the
> other 30 percent attending things merely
> denominated colleges. These poor kids and
> their parents were performing the perpetual
> American quest not for intellect but for
> respectability and status. /T/he number
> of young people really going to college
> will always be about 13 percent. . . .

Is it just possible that Fussell's point may be
right? Writing about his experiences at Ohio State
earlier in this century, James Thurber in <u>My Life
and Hard Times</u> discusses the struggle with the
microscope (Thurber drew the reflection of his own
eye), the stupidity of a football player in an
economics class, and ROTC drill for four years.
Breaking the light tone of the chapter, "University
Days," Thurber observes sourly: "It was a period of
muddy thought and marked, I believe, the decline of
higher education in the Middle West."

However, cultural deprivation is neither private
nor public. At the moment, it is universal, like
ignorance itself. Complaints about the flaws of
"higher learning" have been constant in this century
since Thorsten Veblen. Jacques Barzun's <u>Education in
America</u>, approaching its fiftieth year of publication,
complained insistently about what others should but

don't know, such as the deciphering of Roman numerals or the niceties of meanings of terms such as "replete." Barzun writes resolutely within urban confines and the institutional parameters, despite the books title, of Columbia College.

So too did Upton Sinclair, who autobiographically attacked a still older Columbia for its political reactionaries, poor teaching, and snobbery. At Yale, Robert Penn Warren complained about students' ignorance, especially their poor historical knowledge. One of Warren's predecessors at Yale, William O. Douglas, in Go East, Young Man, had this to say about part of Fussell's magically endowed thirteen percent who attend our national Belve U's.

/In the 1920's/ Yale College was filled with sons of the elite who lived in a warm glow of easy scholarship, easy living, easy work. They were the 'chosen' who in time would run the nation. The college professors dealt kindly with them: they were spoon-fed, coddled, pampered. I early discovered that . . . the Yale College men in my law classes were waiting for someone to fill their heads with knowledge. Yale, in those days, was notorious for being that kind of filling station.

The record of recent decline in academic standards at all levels, however, is irrefutable. The observations made by Professors E. D. Hirsch, Jr., in Cultural Literacy and Alan Bloom in The Closing of the American Mind apply equally to public and private, save for a small minority (often conservatively religious, such as Yeshiva) which have refused to change either their standards or their subject matter over the last twenty years. A few schools, private and public, have maintained their standards in the sciences and humanities. The rest have denatured their courses, reduced faculty, and, through grade inflation, compromised essential standards of academic value and public trust.

At one campus of a state university, the identity of the institution has become so divided that it approaches collegial schizophrenia. While some of the graduates go on to the best dental and medical schools, get into the best and better professional schools (Harvard and Cornell Law, for instance), admission standards and curricula have been eased to retain student enrollments--for funding is based on student numbers. After the turmoil of the early 1970's, this four year college developed undergraduate programs in business, journalism, business education, and other modishly "practical" offerings. Conversely, with consistently declining levels of financial support, nearly all hiring stopped in those courses and departments basic to any reputable institution of higher learning. By 1987, no faculty had been hired by the English Department for fourteen years, by history for twelve, political science for eight, philosophy for ten, foreign languages for nine. Moreover, department hirings were lopsidedly inadequate: for three or four or five faculty retirees, one instructor would be hired as a replacement, given an additional course load with reduced pay. One department hired six part-time instructors, with mixed credentials, to replace three retiring full professors.

On this campus, the effects of this policy of inertia and atrophy are striking. Humanities, arts, and science courses, with fewer or no younger faculty, are less vital and less attractive to students, who, at any rate, pursue their own Gresham's Law of Academic Debasement. This, for instance, is a semester's course of study for three college room-mates, whose parents are lawyers, urban high school teachers, and accountants:

> Basic Programming
> Principles of Accounting
> Organizational Communication
> Nutrition for the Athlete
> Contemporary Square Dance
> Musicians Talk about Music
> Mathematics of Finance

Even though two of these courses did not carry the full three hours of semester credit, the mishmash is mind hobbling.

Like many college and high school students these days, these three were reluctant readers. None of them read a serious newspaper or magazine; only one had read a book in the past year, Hollywood Wives by Jackie Collins. The other two students had no plans to read any books, other than text books, at any time. None of their college courses in fact required the reading of a book, or a series of books (such as semi-popular ones on economics by our own contemporary "Adam Smith" or on science and biology by Stephen Jay Gould, etc.). They left the TV on for most of the day and night, reserving a time every weekday for the soap "General Hospital."

This is, of course, an extreme example of student apathy and malfeasance. Most students at this state institution do not seek such a confused menu in "earning" their degree, which, if pursued in the Jackie Collins Core Curriculum, will be just as valueless as Fussell asserts.

Nonetheless, other problems at this state campus are manifold. The same forces which drove the institution to increase its "professionalism" dictated other changes. In the early 1970's, the state decreased by twenty percent the number of liberal arts and science courses required for its education majors. Aggravating this decline of standards, departments such as education, educational psychology, physical education, business, contrived over two hundred hours of spurious "liberal arts" courses. At the same time, the traditional disciplines worked against their own values and heritage. A student can, then, take "liberal arts" courses in the usual departments, such as English or philosophy or history (the already mentioned "History through Film," "Baseball Fiction," "Lyrics of Rock and Roll," or the oxymoronic "Business Ethics"). The same scholastic pilgrim may, and usually does, further adulterate his semester's work with a course in "The Civil Rights of Students and Teachers" (offered in two semesters for six hours total credit), "Bilingual Schooling in the U.S." (no 'foreign' language required), or "Introduction to Foundations." Home Economics, not to be outdone, offers six semester hours of "History of Costume I," "History of Costume II," and thirty-three other "liberal arts" courses from the "History of Furniture" to "Development through Play," the last perhaps an unwitting description of many present-day colleges.

This may be the warp of academic debasement, but as already noted, the woof of this botched tapestry may be provided by traditional departments themselves. In a national drive for survival, college English departments have abandoned Shakespeare, Chaucer, Dickens and George Eliot for the comma splice, or exist for the teaching of rock lyrics, the literature of advertising, or other pop-debasements, such as undergraduate courses in journalism. A once proud department of twenty years ago offering four courses in Shakespeare and forty hours of courses at the upper level now finds itself mired in simple survey courses of mediocre quality, and a large program in remediation, that is, teaching the parts of speech and the simplest of writing skills. The department's upper division courses have been cut by more than fifty per cent.

Another graphic example of this trend exists in the college's music department. True to recent form, over a fifteen year period one instructor has been hired after the retirement of four professors. In the rush to the popular and the practical, the department developed a program in the "music industry." Its course "Music and the Marketplace" enjoys "liberal arts" status. Ten years ago the most popular courses in the department were taught by a harpsichordist and scholar of baroque music; now the most popular course is in rock and roll. Moreover, students enrolling in the "music industry" program often don't know the rudiments of music itself, so that essential courses in the discipline have devolved to the barest rudiments, such as teaching sight-reading. "F-A-C-E" and other primitive demotics of the treble and bass have replaced harmony, theory, and solfeggio. The college is the proud owner of forty Steinway pianos, but only a few students of the instrument survive, and only a part-time piano instructor remains.

But to return to the most essential of the academic crafts, reading and writing. Neither on this campus is in good order, and this despite more courses in writing offered by the English department, with large gobbets of "communication" developed by the faculty in speech, the new programs in "business communication" and a major in "communications." Nearly all departments, even the most traditional, shirk the assignment of written papers. A history professor justified not assigning any written work in his classes: "It only encourages them to plagiarize." More than one major in this department graduates without having written a single serious essay in the discipline.

On a college campus with about the same miscegenation of mixed standards, this was the finding of an informal survey--all errors intact:

> An advanced writing class answered several rudimentary questions about the writing of papers, about what courses required papers, and how many courses required use of the library and the use of reserve books. Most of the students were seniors or juniors. As expected, the weakest writers, those in the professional curricula and those with the least ability to read competently, did the least writing. An education major said that 'some course require writing, most don't.' Business majors, most of whom have an academic minor in 'business communications,' generally do not use the library for their assignments, nor do they read reserve books. One senior summed it up: "Generally my courses do not require the

use of the library.' She was succinct in answering the related question: 'I rarely use reserve books.' On this same matter, another countered, 'Are you serious?' He had never used this section of the library. Another senior wrote: "Most courses do not use books on reserve--courses with papers to write involves using the library.' Several other answers also used fractured grammatical responses--perhaps because the answers weren't considered very important. One senior business major wrote that 'about 3 times I've used reserve book,' because 'generally my courses don't require library.' However, a 'sophmore' said that use of the library was 'generally true if want background material.'

So, what is to be done? Bucking the trend, all of the speakers at this conference call for a return to the basic disciplines as the best preparation for the professions and for life. But what if the departments in the universities and colleges have so befouled their own nests that no primitive "true" meaning any longer exists? This very danger is raised by one of the participants, who observes that the structure of academic departments may be inimical to positive change. The same speaker says that "academic humanists must be flexible and choose to assert themselves, even if that means consolidation of resources, even if that means changing comfortable administrative structures, before choices are forced on them, or, worse, before the power to choose is denied."

More radical solutions, though, could be implemented, beginning with a more demanding and structured accreditation process of public and private institutions of higher learning. Now conducted by committees of a few professors and administrators who stay on a campus for a few days, assess the material presented to them by carefully selected faculty and administrators, and read the artfully edited college reports (some departments write them so poorly that they have to be rewritten by literate members of English departments). The visitation is a collegial and usually genial happening, and little if any academic value is transmitted. These periodic assessments by such organizations as the Middle States Association of Colleges and Schools should be more tightly focused and defined, with the time of assessment doubled or even tripled, with the members of the committee looking at the book lists for courses, written criteria for course conduct, and the credentials of faculty members and administrators. More than the present one or two students should be interviewed to determine their temper and the demands the institution makes on them. Finally, the reviewing committee should make specific and pointed suggestions for the improvement of each campus, with deadlines for their implementation. If the goals are not met, the institution should be censured and lose its accreditation.

The education major as we now know it should be abolished; each future teacher should have a dual major in two academic disciplines, or a major in an academic discipline with two minors in conventional and conservative academic subjects.

Reading and writing in all college courses must be implemented, with a writing examination being part of the admissions process. The reading of books in the subjects, not mere text-books, must also be required.

It is also long past time for the state and federal governments to pull their funding from institutions which are counter-productive, which lower and frust.ate the standards of learning rather than raising and fulfilling them. State universities must more actively monitor the quality of their tax-subsidized institutions. The same goes for the federal subsidies. No funds should be spent on weak institutions which refuse to improve their standards, and no student should receive guaranteed loans to attend such institutions.

At a talk given in 1987 to the National Press Club in Washington, D.C., Lynne V. Cheney, Chair of the National Endowment for the Humanities, spoke with some fervor about the failings of American education at the junior and high school level: few students knew who Willa Cather is or what she wrote, not very many could correctly identify the date of Columbus's discovery of the New World, almost no one knew the dates, even within a half-century, of the 1861-1865 American Civil War, etc., etc.

But at the end of her talk, Cheney disappointingly said that there was no intervention planned by the Federal Government. Any attempt at improvement must be "voluntary."

Matters at all levels of education in the United States have gotten to such a pass that "voluntarism" is an evasion. The proposal for a more hearty and demanding evaluation of standards at the higher levels of education is not, of course, a panacea, but only a modest beginning for improvement and a return to standards of the most basic and honest kind.

Why take such difficult and demanding positions?

A student of mine from some years ago visited the campus as I was editing this book. He now lives in suburbia, owns a home, drives a new car, plays golf several times a week, and is a bank vice-president. The explanation for his success? "I know how to read and write!" These two happy and basic skills he learned as a major in one of the disciplines of the humanities.

The very real danger, observable on most campuses, is that the rush to professional programs has actually maimed their student victims, making them less rather than more employable, lessened rather than nurtured their skills.

And these are the pernicious tendencies that must be arrested at all levels of American education, high and low, public or private.

THREE-DIMENSIONAL EDUCATION

John E. Smith

Education, like religion and party politics, is an explosive topic about which many people have strong differences of opinion. I believe that this is just as it should be, for these topics concern what an ancient Greek philosopher called "the things that matter most," the ideals determining the course and worth of life itself. A genuine cause for alarm would exist if the vigor of the discussion about education should cease and be replaced by apathy or indifference. In this regard even the one who expresses views in a dogmatic way is superior to the one who is indifferent; the dogmatist at least cares.

It should not be difficult to understand why education or, more properly, teaching and learning, should engage so much of our attention. What happens in our educational institutions at all levels determines, for the most part, the make-up of the new generation and with it the future of national life, even of civilization itself. The case of Socrates forcefully underscores the point, even if the outcome was tragic in itself. He antagonized those who opposed him not primarily because of his alleged disrespect for the gods of popular religion, but because he exhorted the young to seek self-knowledge, to think for themselves, to learn how to discern what is true as against what is deceptive and false, and, most important, to seek as guides for human conduct those virtues which mark out the "good of the soul," making it possible for people to live together in civil society. Socrates, in short, was a teacher, par excellence, but he was k gadfly to his contemporaries because, instead of focusing on the acquisition of information about the world and the development of skills and crafts, he insisted on the

1

absolute importance of the ethical quality of human life. Without, he argued, the power of wisdom, of courage, of temperance, and above all, justice, there can be no civilized life, individual or social.

In my title, I refer to "three-dimensional" education. I mean to set that off from an education of but two dimensions and to do so with the help of the Socratic insight. Time and again the aims of education have been stated as the stocking of the mind with knowledge, including the development of the ability to think clearly, and the preparing of a person to engage in some vocation or profession as a means of livelihood. But important as these two dimensions undoubtedly are, the third and far most important dimension is missing--the aim and task of developing civilized persons, or those who have the self-knowledge, the self-control, the sense of responsibility and the ideals and concerns that make it possible for them to live in a civilized society committed to the realization of freedom and justice. Without this third dimension, all of our knowledge is vain, and our vocations and professions fall to the level of mere competitive struggles for money and power.

Civilization depends on the existence of civilized persons; that is the fact. The loss of the third dimension in our educational thought and practice is at the root of our modern difficulties in every region of life. The urgent question is, Can this lost dimension of education be recovered? I believe that the answer is yes, but that answer has to be prefaced by an if--if we can succeed in making the humanities come alive and fulfill their essential role, which is, and has always been, contributing to the development of civilized persons. Man is both a knower and a maker, but it takes little historical knowledge to become aware of the fact that all knowledge and all activity can be put to evil and destructive ends. Unless human beings come to see themselves as responsible beings--man is the only animal capable of answering for himself and his deeds--the question of worthwhile ends and goals will not arise. But if it does, we are lost if we have no knowledge of or insight into the ideals that make civilization possible. The vast resources of the humanistic studies can provide this insight and thus form the missing third dimension in our educational venture.

Too often it has been supposed that before we can make plain the role of the humanities in liberal education, we must first define them. Nothing could be further from the truth. As Kant pointed out long ago, the only study that can begin with definitions is mathematics; all other inquiries may aim at definitions only as a possible outcome of having plumbed the field. There is no dispute about what constitutes the humanities--literature, the language, art, philosophy, history, religion, and I would include science as a human achievement--the task is to express their significance in terms that highlight their contribution to human development. To this end, I propose the thesis that the humanities are "the mirror of man," the glass in which we see reflected both what man has been and visions of what he may become. The mirror reflects the actual works of man, the persistent expression of human concerns, experiences, desires, needs, and aspirations across a great variety of cultures and civilizations. But more than that, the mirror also reflects an ideal dimension in the form of visions of the good life, the values to be pursued and the evils to be avoided. Every theory of "human nature" embraces both poles in that every grasp of what man is is intertwined with some image of what human life ideally should be. The mirror, in short, reflects both the actual and the ideal so that when we look into it we achieve not only self-understanding, but some conception of what we should strive for if we are to conduct our lives as human beings.

I set for myself two tasks--first, to speak generally about what I shall call the "three lessons" to be learned from the mirror, and, second, I shall attempt to illustrate from my experience in the program of the National Humanities Institute at Yale

3

and in summer seminars sponsored by the National Endowment for the Humanities for people in the professions the vital contributions of the humanities in liberal education to the resolution of some of the most perplexing problems we face in the areas of law, medicine, education, mass media, civil rights, and social and economic priorities. We cannot, in the nature of the case, speak of having in hand ready-made solutions, but we can help to develop persons who will view these problems from the perspective of humane visions and the values involved and who will not forget that regardless of the size and remoteness of modern organizations and institutions, the focus has always to be on people and their welfare.

Stated briefly, the three lessons taught by the mirror of man are, first, the discovery and the recovery of the complex of ideals and norms upon which our Western civilization has actually been founded and which at least until the erosions brought about by skepticism and nihilism have made life worth living; second, since we see ourselves in the mirror, what it reflects provides an essential opportunity for self-criticism and the candid perception that being human embraces a considerable capacity for inhumanity and irresponsibility; third, and in some ways most important, the reflection of man in the great imaginative literature of the ages provides an inexhaustible storehouse of vicarious experience, overcoming parochialism and extending our horizons. Before explaining these lessons in some detail, I believe one qualifying word is in order. I do not say that the three contributions singled out exhaust the role of the humanities, nor do I believe that the school, college, or university can or should be the only institutions responsible for the development of civilized persons. Many more obligations have been thrust upon our educational systems than they can legitimately bear, but I would still insist on the need for education at every level to recover what I have called the third dimension, which is in fact a matter of moral education in the broadest sense.

4

Many young people remain largely ignorant of the ideals that have guided and shaped the civilization of which they are a part. We have so exaggerated what is true, namely, that values cannot be "taught" after the fashion of mathematics or chemistry, that we fail even to teach students about the values that have in fact sustained our civilization. Through the teaching of history, philosophy, and religious studies, each new generation needs to be made aware of both our debt to and the contemporary importance of the moral and religious sources upon which our lives have depended--the norms of justice, mercy, righteousness, and love derived from the Judeo-Christian tradition; the ideals of truth and of virtue bequeathed by the Graeco-Roman traditions; the convictions of the Enlightenment concerning inalienable rights, human equality, and the need for representative forms of government; the experience of democracy and free institutions. Even more importantly, we have failed, largely because of a fear of bias and partisanship in a pluralistic society, to focus on the reality of the moral situations that constantly confront us so that the ethical dimension is obscured and moral sensitivity erodes. A recent book by Milton Konvitz, Judaism and the American Idea, furnishes an excellent example of the manner in which the faith of an ancient tradition can be revivified and brought to bear on such problems as the rule of law, democracy, religious freedom, and human rights. I choose one telling example from this book. The ancient belief that man is a creature of God, says Konvitz, stands as a bulwark against any creed, political or otherwise, that would envisage man as basically a creation or merely an organ of the state. That ancient belief belongs to our Western heritage and should be known to every educated and civilized person. Why is such a piece of knowledge less important than the great storehouse of knowledge imparted in the study of nations, parliaments, physical systems, industrial corporations, primitive tribes, and social orders? The answer is surely that it is of equal if not greater importance in the end than all the factual knowledge we have because it concerns the humanity of man in opposition

5

to those who see man as no more than a thing among other things. The moral and religious roots of our civilization should receive no less attention in our education than the study of galaxies, genetics, or constitutions. The sad fact is that study of those roots is often neglected entirely.

The second lesson to be learned by looking into the mirror of the humanities--that it provides us with an essential opportunity for self-criticism and honest appraisal of our inhumanity--is likely to come as a surprise to all who associate the "humanities" with the idealized universal man of the Renaissance. The truth is that the very reason why we need to be concerned with the development of civilized persons is the presence in all human beings of tendencies and motives that work against the preservation of civilization. Our capacities for irresponsibility, prejudice, self-deception, personal and social immorality, are manifest on every page of written history. To ignore this dark side of man or to attempt to explain it away be placing the responsibility for it everywhere else but in man himself is basically dishonest and beneath the dignity of the one being who is answerable for himself and his deeds. Examples from the literature of the humanities are as numerous as the stars and, fortunately, much closer. Where shall we find a more candid portrait of man the political animal than in Machiavelli's The Prince, and who can equal his ruthless realism of insight into the wiles, the machinations, and the dissembling necessary to gain and hold political power? Machiavelli has often been attacked for seeming, at least, to condone both the methods and the cynicism of Realpolitik, but surely he is to be commended for holding up the mirror in which can be seen the stark realities of politics and the human will to power.

At an even more fundamental level, consider the consummate skill with which Dostoevsky portrayed the tragic dialectic of human freedom in his sketch of the "Grand Inquisitor." Seeing himself as vastly different from a stone or a star, man strives for freedom and self-determination both in the beliefs he

6

holds and the deeds he performs. The cherished freedom, however, is burdened with care, responsibility, and risk; too often the burden of it becomes so onerous that we stand ready to abrogate our freedom or to delegate it to another, and there are always those who are eager to usurp all the freedom we seek to escape, thus turning us into bondsmen entirely given unto the hands of an alien authority. No merely conceptual, philosophical analysis of the ambiguity of human freedom could possibly match in vividness and persuasiveness Dostoevsky's dramatic presentation of human frailty in the face of the awesome demands of being free. One need not spell out the lesson in didactic fashion; it is enough to insist that a civilized person needs to be confronted with these humbling truths about mankind. As Pascal pointed out, there is a glory in man's reaching for infinity through the power of his mind, but there is also the bitter truth than man is the being who can dissemble, who tries to hide and escape the responsibility of his freedom. Nietzsche was right in saying that there is something hypocritical in man's claim to be in pursuit of truth when he is not honest about himself and his own situation.

The third lesson from the mirror has to do with the almost limitless range of vicarious experience opened up to us in imaginative literature, history, and the arts. We are all greatly limited in what we can directly live through and experience for ourselves. But our horizons can be vastly extended to an understanding of, a sympathy for, and participation in other cultures and civilizations through the humanistic studies. Consider the vicarious experience of the grandeur and the terror of human life as portrayed by Tolstoy in War and Peace; the depths of human folly and human aspiration depicted by Dante in the Divine Comedy; the quest for integral selfhood so brilliantly set forth by Goethe in his treatment of the Faust legend. Or, closer to home, consider the doors and windows opened by such writers as Faulkner and Eudora Welty on American southern culture. Reading them gives a vivid sense

7

of "being there without being there," which is what vicarious experience essentially is.

How are future generations of Americans to understand and participate in the many foreign cultures that a shrinking world demands that we encounter when our experience and horizons remain parochial? Not the least of the tragic aspects of the massive tragedy that was Vietnam is to be found in our equally massive ignorance of the culture, the religion, and the ethos of the people involved. The fact is that not everyone in the world thinks of human life exclusively as we do in economic and military terms. But unless our educational system can recover what I have called the third dimension, matters of this sort will not be considered, and the horizon of the next generation will turn out to be as limited as our own.

I come now to some practical considerations-- the humanities at work, as it were--that point the way to what can be done in the way of revitalizing the humanistic studies. As I pointed out earlier, I am relying here on experience gained at the National Humanities Institute in New Haven and in summer seminars sponsored by the National Endowment for the Humanities. The essential first step is that of overcoming the isolation of the various fields of study from each other through a cooperative approach aimed at restoring the integrity of experience and of the world, which in themselves are innocent of the selectivity and abstraction upon which all specialized inquiry is based. Scientists long ago discovered that problems that might prove insoluble for a single investigator may ultimately be resolved by many individuals attacking the problem from several sides. Students and teachers of the humanities can profit from the practice of the natural scientists. By focusing attention on specific problems, historical periods, value conflicts, social, political, and economic issues, interdisciplinary courses can be developed that require the combined knowledge and teaching skills of those in several different fields of study. Consider an art historian who comes to the

8

realization that Western perceptions of Oriental peoples, their appearances, customs, values, and so forth, have been to a large extent determined by the sketches, drawings, and paintings made by the artists who participated in the great voyages of discovery that first brought us into contact with Eastern peoples. The study and interpretation of these artifacts will obviously require the efforts not only of an art historian, but of geographer, an anthropologist, and perhaps a philosopher and a historian of religion. A course developed to focus on the central theme--the initial perception of new and unfamiliar people and cultures--will not appear to be a course "in" one subject or one "department," because the emphasis will not be on subjects or departments at all but rather on the unifying theme itself, which all participants are attempting to illuminate through the facet of the topic assigned to them.

From the standpoint of the teachers involved, an enterprise of this sort is most exciting because one is relating what one knows to something that transcends all the participants; this is very different from routine and often stultifying discussion with "professionals" in the same field. From the standpoint of the teachers involved, an enterprise of this sort is most exciting because one is relating what one knows to something that transcends all the participants: this is very different from routine and often stultifying discussion with "professionals" in the same field. From the standpoint of students, what could be more important than their witnessing cooperative scholarship at work and, in the case of this particular example, discovering the existence of prejudice, stereotype, and misconception in their own images of people from other cultures?

Examples could be multiplied, but the point will remain the same. All the important landmarks, artifacts, events, and so forth, of civilization are too rich and complex to be treated from the vantage point of a single field of inquiry. The proper study of the works of Shakespeare, for example, is not to

9

be accomplished from the field of "English" alone. Needed as well will be the insights of historians, philosophers, sociologists; and, since students cannot be expected to work out the necessary syntheses themselves, scholars will have to work together among themselves to provide them.

I wish now to call attention to another vital role to be played by the humanities in connection with perplexing issues facing professional people in the course of carrying on their work. On two occasions in recent years I have conducted a seminar for those in the professions of law, medicine, journalism, education, and public administration on the topic of "The Ethical Dimension in Contemporary Society." I choose two incidents to illustrate my point. A doctor in charge of a sophisticated neonatal clinic in the mIdwest indicated that more than once a week, in consultation with parents, guardians, clergyman and other physicians, he is called upon to decide whether to remove infants with various birth defects from life-sustaining apparatus. He confessed that although this is his responsibility, he often finds himself at a loss to set forth the rationale for his decision, and needs an opportunity to talk with philosophers, students of ethics and religion in order to gain insight and perspective on his own activity. And the striking fact is that at this point he lamented his failure during the period of his own liberal, as distinct from professional education to pay more attention to the entire spectrum of the humanities and those concerns about the bases of civilized life that I have called the third dimension in education.

A second example involves the legal profession. A member of the seminar not a lawyer opened the discussion by asking whether lawyers are ever determined in their work by a concern for the "truth" or "justice" of the case at hand, or whether they see their task as simply that of representing an "interest" in opposition to another interest regardless of such ideal considerations. A young lawyer responded by saying that he entered the profession

with a strong sense of obligation to justice, but soon
discovered that the tide was against him and that
more often than not the chief concern is to represent
an interest well and "win" in court. A seasoned
jurist countered by saying that it is the task of the
lawyer to present the case and not to judge it and
still less to prejudge it; consequently he cannot
determine the "truth" or the "right" of the case in
advance. The full depth of the ethical dimension of
the legal profession opened up before us. To whom
and to what is the lawyer responsible, and what is
he to do when his responsibility to the client comes
in conflict with his responsibilities both to himself
and to his society? We soon found ourselves where
the seminar had started--a discussion of the trial of
Socrates and his condemnation, among other things,
of the rhetoricians who aimed at making the worse
case seem the better. The striking fact was that all
participants agreed that the underlying questions of
values, priorities, responsibilities, and obligations are
inescapable. Once again there was the lament that
over-emphasis on "practical" subjects thought to be
essential for professional training had crowded out
those "impractical" courses in the humanistic studies.

The plain truth is that the matters with which
the humanities deal are inescapable because they
concern us as human beings. If we are to remain
civilized and succeed in preserving civilization, our
liberal education must recover that third dimension
which requires us to come to terms with "the things
that matter most."

Questions

*One basis for liberal education is the standard for
making decisions. Can those decisions be ethical if
based on ignorance, or merely on the knowledge of
one special subject? As change occurs at an even
more rapid pace, based largely on scientific discoveries,
what is the relevance of former ethical decision-
making?

First of all, though our world is much more technological than it was before, there is more reluctance among college students to take advantage of those scientific areas. So I'm against simple criticism, simple degradations of the technological dimension. We have to understand more about what technology is and does, but at the same time, we must not give up the critical judgment about science. That's one point I want to make.

Years ago, Dewey pointed out that the dazzling successes of science and even the power of a kind of scientism have done a very great deal to erode the authority of many moral and religious convictions that were powerful over the centuries. Even Dewey could say, on Tuesdays, Wednesdays, and Saturdays, that science couldn't replace, totally, older ethical systems, and the other days he'd talk as though it could. Now, knowledge is always necessary. Nobody lives in accordance with the kinetic theory of gases. But to turn the question around: if there hadn't been a conviction of truth owned by no man or no nation, we wouldn't have science in the first place. The ancient scientists knew this. It's only contemporary researchers who get paid rather than to search for the truth.

So the values were there. Now they have eroded, and to make it worse, the first thing we see that makes everything so difficult is that there are new issues involved for which there are no obvious precedents. It's a little over twenty years ago that the amniotic fluid used to be discarded, but to use the language of our contemporaries, the information in that fluid is "unbelievable." If we go into the area of biomedical ethics, so many of the problems that we have to speak about are not simply to be dealt with by finding precedents from the past, but involve the complex, constant reusing of old ideas in situations that we didn't meet with before. That's what I mean by the double bind. Here we are a time when ethical sensitivity is not exactly at a high ebb. So we're caught in a situation of considerable erosion at the same time we're facing issues that

12

cannot simply be dealt with by precedent. Nonetheless we have to get into the areas themselves to see just what the ethical difficulties are.

*You mentioned the achievements derived from the seminars of the National Humanities Institute attended by professionals. Can younger, even much younger undergraduates integrate ideas from different disciplines?

Put it this way. Is it necessary that these two things we're describing should exclude each other, the specific subject and its relation to other disciplines? I agree that we have two traditions that symbolically agree. Both Plato and Ezekial, in very different ways, had the idea that people rally shouldn't study deep mysteries, philosophical or religious, before they were thirty. This obviously is another era! Yet there's a truth in that because, for example, a lot of discussion we may engage in with students borders on things they don't necessarily experience. But I would never say this in the classroom. We must never say that we are referring to an experience which students don't yet have. That is very, very dangerous ice to be on, lest they think we know something that they don't know. But the way I would put it would be this: it is true that there are things we will talk about that people will not yet have had an opportunity to understand in terms of what they've done. Yet, on the other hand, we have to take seriously that these same people will come and say, "Look, when Socrates talked about the unexamined life not being worth living," we all have at the very least a chance at reflective comparison, alternative ways of justifying a certain way of proceeding. We start thinking about the humanistic traditions.

As for the older students in the NEH seminar, I found a certain kind of anti-intellectual drift. They were all a bit intimidated by having to go back again and read some passages from John Stewart Mill about Utilitarianism and the calculus of pleasure and pain or Kant, who says in discussing the adage, Honesty

13

is the best policy: honesty is better than any policy; beware of those fellows to whom honesty is a policy. However, the older students read at their level of concern once they recovered from the sense that someone was putting them back in school.

At any age it's difficult if you're up against the kind of mind that says, "Well, now look. Let's not talk about any of these fine distinctions. Let's just get down to it." Anyone who doesn't want the fine distinctions and thinks he should "just get down to it" doesn't know what he's talking about. Knowledge can't be dealt with haphazardly. It must be dealt with with some precision. However, I'm hoping there's room for both sides of what we're saying.

If we've had the situation where we are engaged in continuing education or adult education, there surely is one thing about talking to people about their experience. They may not know a lot of things; they may have forgotten them. But believe me, you do have the interest and concern and at least the root in experience. You never are put in the position, as with the contemporary college generation, of having to carry on both sides of the dialogue. If I'm going to slay Hume's theory of causation, I've first got to set it up. I've got to take both sides. I've got to make a dragon and then kill it. That gets to be rather disconcerting in a sense that education has been reduced to a monologue. Only one side is in operation.

*Perhaps bringing alive the past by the humanities has been too timid. What does presenting a subject on Monday, Wednesday, Friday do to really impress itself on the students? What will help students grasp the subject more completely?

Certainly we have to communicate some sense from the outset that it makes a difference to us, what we're talking about. I'm afraid that too often that doesn't happen. So if students don't think that what you're talking about makes a difference, if they don't get the impression that it makes a difference

14

to us, we may go to our graves and metaphorically
dig it first. I have, for example, to try to engage
the questions at the point where people are puzzled
in a philosophy course. I've got to find out what
those frowns mean. Nine times out of ten, maybe
ninety-nine out of a hundred, the kind of problem
that somebody comes across with turns out to be
pervasive. I don't know if it is a narcissism of the
time (I doubt it because in my experience of
teaching over thirty years, it was always like this).
Mainly, people think that their problems are unique.
If they dare indicate there is something they don't
understand or don't know they'll be marked forever
as idiosyncratic. But as a matter of fact, more often
than not those problems are the ones that all the
others are worried about, but they are afraid to
speak. So I do think that we have to try to goad
them into daring to use, let's say, a perplexity.

Somebody's reading William James' Varieties of
Religious Experience, and he comes in and says,
"Look, that can't be right. He emphasizes so
completely the absolute individual and his solitude.
What about the religious community?" So I say,
"There's your topic." You see, the student had the
impression that all he had to do was something he
wasn't interested in because it was an assignment.
What that usually means is that students go into the
library and get a lot of books on the subject from
the shelves and put passages together. Then they
put a bibliography in the back. This is called a
"research paper," which as we know contains zero
thought. Now we can get the person to hook the
perplexity into writing. So it's not just a matter of
people being able "to write," but the capacity to
analyze and synthesize. We've got to integrate the
thinking and the expression, to overcome that
nonsense: 'Oh, don't pay attention to the way I'm
saying this. Get my good ideas underneath." We
must say, 'Well, I've been looking underneath and
don't see them."

*One of the problems in your presentation is that

15

you blanket students with labels and stereotypical reactions which define them as objects--

No, that's precisely what I don't mean. What we must try to do is to keep people thinking, to latch on to some individual perplexity, some problem they're prepared to talk and write about. When it comes to the official assignment. they say, "Well, this is very difficult; you didn't tell us what to write about." The answer is easy: "Well, that's part of what the book is all about. We've already discussed the topic."

However, we are responsible in a sense in categorizing students. Given the necessity of an institution, its structure of curriculum, we are bound to wind up with courses, assignments, grading. So there's a sense in which one has always to continue to surmount the system; but yet, if I may come back on the other side, let students not overlook the extent to which they depend on the everlasting arms of the system. I was in Paris in the sixties when those paving stones were hurled. One of the things that interested me about that revolt, and it did receive very little emphasis in the press, was that the French students wanted a central administration like American colleges that would keep the professors coming to class! At times they don't have to be there; they own their own endowed chairs. I was very much struck by that. In the midst of all the revolutionary talk, what the French students really wanted was an establishment that would have this power to organize, to make it reasonably certain the Professor X would be on the reservation often enough to answer questions.

So I don't want to be identified with having described all students in some simple way as not thinking. We're all capable of that inactivity.

*Aren't students drawn in so many different directions by television, social life, that institutions of higher learning have less monopoly of students' attention? Don't we have to consider the environment in and

16

outside the institution and take those changes into account?

I sympathize with that, but I also like to be treated like a person. One of Dewey's main points is that interest is a fundamental relationship that has to be engendered with regard to the subject. I feel I have the certain responsibility to try to engender my own concern, my enthusiasm for this important subject. I don't know how to quantify this, but I'd like to be met half way!

It's a mistake for instance to encourage students to delay final commitments to courses until nearly the end of the semester. This provides infinite possibilities of postponement.

*What's the underlying assumption that led to this?

First of all, we've made education into an industry. Secondly, an industry turns out products. Products are valuable. So we have the idea that students pay money to get a commodity which presumably I have, which I'm willing to give up for a price. To put it at its worst, I deliver this to the customer with the least possible discomfort and disarrangement of personal convenience. Now the whole ideal of a commodity, purchasable for a price, and the whole grading business that goes along with that, makes it very difficult for us to educate.

I had years ago--if I may tell this anecdote--a run-in with the Internal Revenue Service and its inspector, a former teacher. An unhappy combination for a taxpayer! I had wanted to make a few deductions. I was the director of graduate studies and I threw some parties for the incoming students that were at my own expense. There was no budget for that, and I proposed to make some deductions with evidence. "Oh," the inspector said, "No, you can't do that because you don't sell a product." "Oh," I said, "I agree with you, but culture is against you."

17

*You place a good deal of emphasis on the humanities. What about the sciences? Aren't they equally important?

Yes, without question. If I may offer a piece of evidence that I like to point to because it's been very important for me in my relations with my scientific colleagues: I used to give a seminar called "Science and Human Values" in which I tried to talk about some of the issues raised by increasing technology. I spent a good deal of time on that, and you'll find a piece I wrote called "Scientific Outlook and a Scientific Enterprise" the students published in the Yale scientific magazine a few years ago. I tried to distinguish, and this is a job that a humanist should at least put his hand to, the basic enterprise of the sciences from a more generalized, yet scientific outlook on things because the sciences do not add themselves up. So I think that to talk about "a scientific outlook" has to qualify as metaphysics.

One of the reasons I did this is that science should not be made to bear the responsibility for some of the dubious claims made in its behalf by people who are not involved in science at all and who beat the drum against religion or ethics. They invoke the name of science because of its authority. But I have to make some distinctions here. It's more difficult to get the cooperation of people in the natural sciences because they often are so much engaged in other research work of their own. But I certainly would want to strongly urge, and I do as a student advisor, that students should not escape into subject like Jungian psychology instead of physics.

One other thing--largely because philosophers stopped doing the job they should do and got too much involved in minutiae, like the meaning of the, the big issues are taken over by other people. Half the scientists writing are doing so as philosophers telling us about the nature and destiny of man.

To put it another way, thirty or forty years ago philosophers were intimidated because people, either in the sciences or those speaking on their behalf, said, in effect, "It's all clear that science means a steady advance. The history of science is the history of victory over past errors; whereas you fellows in philosophy not only haven't discovered anything new, but you don't even agree on what Plato said." So one had the image of a clear, steady advance in science, and over in philosophy there was a mess. Now the situation isn't quite like that. Science is more of a "mess" these days and is in a good deal of flux and reflection on fundamental questions. On the other side, philosophy isn't all that chaotic. There are a very great many people in the world, but there are only about eight or nine viable philosophical alternatives. So it would follow from a little evidence that at least ten philosophers somewhere agree!

HUMANITIES AND THE MEDICAL PROFESSION
Richard P. Schmidt, M.D.

In February 1977, the State University of New York Senate met in Syracuse and I made some remarks concerning the appointment of Dr. Bruce Dearing as University Professor of the Humanities in Health Sciences assigned to our campus. Some thought it a bit unusual that a professor of English literature, former Dean, University President and Academic Vice-Chancellor would be so chosen to join the academic community of a medical center. Some of my remarks explored the idea of humanizing medical education, of bringing the insights of the humanities into medical studies related to the nature of the human experience. I also expanded upon the idea that these insights would help the tyro physician establish concepts of social role, and to be better able to consider social insights about the meaning of life and death. In short, I believed then, as I believe now, that we in medicine must engage in a meaningful conversation with those from other disciplines to gain the wisdom necessary for the rational use of an expanded science and technology. I also expressed the feeling that the self could be strengthened and placed within the social context if we could infuse the scientific education of our students with the knowledge of the philosopher, the ethicist, and the poet or historian.

I can claim no originality for these ideas. Many other medical colleges had already established departments or programs dealing with that which we may term the liberal arts. A considerable impetus was the formation of the Society of Health and Human Values and the publication of a new journal, The Journal of Medicine and Philosophy for that society by the University of Chicago Press. The editor of this publication, Edmund D. Pellegrino, a former colleague of ours in the State University, is the newly appointed President of Catholic University of America.

My own interest was further increased by our students and their development of a successful student led program entitled, Humanistic Approaches to Health Care.

I might add that the appointment of Professor Dearing appears to be one of the best we have made in my eight years in Syracuse. Let me give one brief example. Students in medical school are exposed to death on their first day of classes by being assigned to a cadaver in the gross anatomy course. As you might expect, this provokes a considerable anxiety. The faculty of the Department of Anatomy now utilize this experience constructively to begin the student's consideration of death. Professor Dearing participates actively, reviewing with them some of the history of dissection and of attitudes associated with it through the ages. Anxiety appears to be lessened and the students begin their medical career with thoughts about the meaning of death and value of life.

As a medical educator, I must also be concerned with the processes of education taking place prior to the student's entry into medical school. The norm for our entries is about as follows: age 22-25 years, education 16 years (including four years in college), grade-point average 3.5 or above, major--biological sciences or chemistry. Professor Summers could cite a similar level of achievement for those who enter the law. We receive about 4000 applications each year and admit 150 of these into medical school. Those of you who teach at the undergraduate level are well aware of the intensity of competition for entry into medical, dental, law, and other upper level professional schools. It is a very visible process, brought into critical focus by court decisions as in the case of Bakke vs the University of California. Nationally, almost two-thirds of those who apply to medical school are rejected in spite of the fact that

21

the available first year places have almost doubled in the 10 years since 1968. We share with others the challenges of affirmative action, political pressures, government regulations and such vexing problems as curriculum innovation mandated by law.

In these circumstances it is no wonder that I keep our admissions process under close scrutiny. I am impressed by the fair-minded approach by those who have accepted the responsibility of serving in this important function, although I will concede the process is imperfect and I grieve for those who might be well-qualified but fail to gain acceptance. This, however, is not my purpose in mentioning admissions--at least here. Rather, I direct my attention to those aspects of the pre-professional education which permit a few judgments.

First of all, I am greatly disturbed by that which I hear concerning the stereotype of the pre-medical student. This is clearly expressed in a characterization found by my daughter when she was an undergraduate debating with herself about a career in music, mathematics, or in medicine. Pre-medical students were characterized as a "gray, homogeneous mass of compulsive over-achievers." We also hear of the intensity of grade competition, of cheating, of destruction of reference material and the like. On close examination of actual medical students, I must say, we see but few of these characteristics. I am concerned, however, that we have created an exceptionally unhealthy competition on the part of this group of undergraduates. It is certainly not that group of characteristics we most desire for our future physicians.

As I sometimes sit as an observer with our admissions committee, I am interested in gaining insight into some of the non-quantitative variables which may make the difference between acceptance and rejection, the quantitative variables are of importance--perhaps too much importance. Thus grades and Medical College Aptitude Test scores are attended to with great care, and achievement levels are assigned primacy.

College recommendations are of great importance, and we have developed a feeling for nuances in the letters we receive. Some give us much better evaluations than others. When I was at another institution, for example, at least half of the graduates from a given college were reported as being among the very best students in recent years. These letters were of little value and largely ignored.

Once the grade hurdle has been leapt, the characteristics of a successful applicant are likely to be those of an expanded interest beyond scientific achievement. Thus, we are likely to admit the student with a broader background in liberal studies. Among those I remember from the last several years have been accomplished musicians, published poets, amateur actors, singers, philosophy majors, social science majors, etc. Some of the most attractive medical students I have known satisfied their science requirements as an afterthought in their basic university education.

Some medical schools have experimented with varying acceptance criteria, admitting significant numbers who do not possess the usual high-grade credits in the sciences but who have undergraduate backgrounds in literature, social sciences or other liberal arts and sciences. Under the leadership of George Harrell, such an experiment was tried at the Milton S. Hershey Medical Center of Pennsylvania State University. I understand that this was successful. It may be noteworthy that Hershey is one of those medical schools with an early and well established program in the humanities.

The choice of a professional career within medicine should and must be of concern to the educator. We may not need more physicians but we do need a different distribution by field of specialization and geographic location. Thus, although this issue remains highly controversial, some

23

of use are "pushing" the specialties of primary care, notably family practice. Does the nature of a liberal education influence the decision of a young person to pursue such a career? I do not know the answer to this. Studies have shown that those who choose specialties such psychiatry and family practice are more likely to have had a stronger emphasis in the humanities during their undergraduate years than are those entering more highly specialized fields. This may be more a characteristic of the person than of the curriculum, but it still seems significant.

Before preparing this presentation I did a fair amount of reading. I studied carefully the Report on the Core Curriculum from Harvard. I had even thought of adapting its recommendations to my own perceptions in medical and pre-medical education. I have not and will not do so even though this does appear to be an influential and important document whether or not one agrees with its series of recommendations. I will, however, affirm my agreement on the first element of the proposed core curriculum, "An educated person must be able to think and write clearly and effectively." I sometimes read the essays which an applicant may submit as part of the material to be considered by the Admissions Committee. I suspect that the Committee usually pays but little attention to these. In reading them, I have been shocked at the apparent inability of one of the brightest, highest-achieving groups of college seniors to use the English language. Multiple errors of spelling and the grossest of grammatical lapses are commonplace. A large proportion of the professional life of a physician is spent in written communication with others. As Harvard Core Curriculum advocates, we should "reaffirm the importance of an expository writing program . . . ." The writing of Lewis Thomas certainly demonstrates that scientific thought can be expressed in elegant English prose.

Finally, I would like to return to some of my thoughts on the liberal or humanist, an expert in English literature, a poet, an ethicist and a sometime

24

philosopher to our faculty? I have mentioned my first idea of the development of the concept of self in the professionalization of the student in the context of society. Of equal or greater importance is our need to face the increasing crisis in health care--the expanded and expanding technology, the concern of a value system where the capability of sustaining life may be balanced against our inability or unwillingness to pay the cost social as well as economic. Important ethical decisions must be made, driven in part by increasing concern over costs. Where more needed is the ethicist than in institutional, governmental or personal decisions directed to the question of who will live and who will die based upon an economic rationing of our powerful technology? What of the problems of population control and the emotionally charged question of abortion? What is life as related to consciousness or its quality? How do we deal with the dying human and his or her family? When do we "pull the plug" of mechanical support systems when all qualities of sentient human life have been irretrievably lost from the body? What support does the physician require when faced with some of the newer and more agonizing decisions which have now become part of a long-established practice in ethics? Some of those we now hear of almost daily are concerned with organ transplantation and the determination of death in the potential donor. Human death certainly needs to be defined legally and ethically. In the past, the heart beat was a convenient measure, especially during times when the heart was thought to house the soul. What of the questions raised by the so-called test-tube babies or of cloning? What will be the ethical concerns of inducing suspended life for human preservation for long periods?

I submit that the answers to these questions are not the exclusive domain of medical practice. Ultimate social decisions will be made in a complex matrix, interwoven fabrics, if you will, of religion, the law, economics, politics, ethics--others--each of which may bring its attitudes and interpretation of the human condition. A liberal education, irrespective of professional role, enhances the ability to participate in and to understand the social processes of socially significant decisions, whether the insights come from science, from moral and ethical systems of thought or from the arts.

These thoughts appear to come together in the changes which have been occurring in dealing with the process of death and how we treat the patient and the families of patients who have fatal or potentially fatal illnesses. We are now more open and have less tendency to avoid addressing the problem of death in planning with patient and family. We also have many patients whose lives are prolonged with appropriate management of incurable illness and many others who do not yet know if their potentially fatal disease may be cured or whether they will have short or long remissions. Kubler-Ross and others have greatly expanded our studies and concern over death and dying. Health professions' students may gain insights into attitudes toward death not only from dealing with their own patients and the cold literature of statistical medicine but from past and contemporary literature. A poignant example of this is in Arnold Wesker's play, Love Letters on Blue Paper, a sensitive portrayal of love between a man and a woman. The man was dying of leukemia. The wife communicated her feelings for him in letters, apparently being unable to face direct oral discussion.

To me, the dramatic art form gave a marvelous insight into the thoughts and frustrations of a dying man and of the love of one human being to another. Such insights would never be possible in a lecture and would seldom be as clearly evident even to those engaged in the real life drama. Basically, education in all its forms is an expansion of this human need: communication in all its forms, in art, science, ethics, and the art and science of medicine.

QUESTIONS

*Mortimer Adler not long ago said the problem was that we were anticipating later professional specialization at the undergraduate level, even in the humanities and liberal arts. Would you comment on that?

We do it even before that. Even in high school, specialization is started very early. This should be, if it occurs, balanced with generalization. I half way agree with the half way suggestion that Lewis Thomas made. My own education was done in a very rapid way. I had my baccalaureate in three years, and the medical degree three years later. Because of the war time experience, they were pushing us through very rapidly. I resented not having the leisure to explore at that time in my life. I resented what I missed. At that time, there was the idea that we didn't have the luxury of having people stay in college or medical school an extra year, two years or more, that they were more needed for the national purpose in conducting World War II. But where the balance would lie, I don't know.

However, this is of some importance. We reject some students with straight A averages. I remember one case very specifically which I can disguise enough so that it won't be recognized. A student with an A average applied to medical school and was rejected. He reapplied the following year. During the interim, he had done graduate work in the hard sciences. During his baccalaureate years, he had only two courses outside the sciences. These were two courses in freshman English. Now, this was an institution with a distinguished reputation.

So if you looked at the scores in the four areas of the medical school qualification test, which at that time was science, general knowledge, and two other topics, the applicant knocked the heck out of the sciences and quantitative abilities, and was in the 98th percentile of all students taking the test nationally. However, he was in the lower fortieth percentile of all those students nationally taking the

27

test for general knowledge and other aspects of interpretation. The student was rejected.

So it is perhaps wise to tell the pre-med students not to point themselves so much in this direction, because they are not likely to get into medical school even though we want them to be bright in the sciences.

*What was the nature of student requests for change at the medical school level that you ar familiar with? Were they as radical as some of the changes other students made?

A small group of students, rather hesitatingly at first and unsure of the future implications, wanted to have part of their medical school curriculum concern itself with such things as ethics, the concerns and worries of the future place of the physician in society, and the like. So this led to the student run and oriented program called the "Humanistic Approaches to Health Care." This came before the appointment of Professor Dearing, who, when he came, fit in very nicely with the working of the students. His office is now filled with people working on some of these problems and beginning to do research on what one can gain, in the medical view of the human experience, from literature and other subjects. Thus far, it's all been voluntary, though there's a means to gain credit through the elective system we have.

Parallel with this is a program started recently by a member of the department of philosophy at Le Moyne College, a faculty member at Syracuse University in sociology and social science, and one of our own professors in psychiatry who is the only member of our faculty to receive a grant from the National Endowment for the Humanities for a sabbatical to write a book. They started something called "A Consortium for the Cultural Foundations of Medicine," which is now beginning to offer credit courses for qualified undergraduates, graduate students, and medical students at our three universities. So this is a reinforcement of values very much needed, not just at my age, but at an age when students are undergraduates, when they desire more breadth.

We have noticed since the sixties a change in the attitudes of the students, particularly in the last three or four years. They're a lot more friendly with us now. We can joke a little bit more. We've always had that group of students, the highly selective group who don't confirm to anything before they get in--but once they do get in they're different. But I think they want to be led into a tightening of the requirements for a liberal education at the undergraduate level. Even now, this group is looking back and seeing some of the things they've not had. These are merely anecdotes, perhaps, but a couple of years ago I interviewed a candidate for the faculty who was one of the brightest young people-- "young people"--he was in his upper thirties--one of the brightest young people to come along in a long time. He was one of the college students chosen by Johns Hopkins to enter medical school at the end of the first year of college, one who could finish the baccalaureate degree and medical school in six years. He was deeply resentful of his own curriculum and university experience. He was resentful of his university. He was anxious to get into the program at the time, but in retrospect resentful. He was at, scientifically and clinically, a level where there was no doubt that he would be a department chairman in a major medical school in the United States. So, obviously, he should have had more time and breadth.

*Does merely taking courses in the liberal arts themselves insure breadth, the answers we're seeking for value and cultural meaning? What is needed in restructuring academic requirements? Is the interdisciplinary approach the answer?

I've had both good and bad luck with interdisciplinary courses. We have one, for example, of very high quality, where people come from different disciplines without changing their approach. If this is interdisciplinary, then creative play of two year olds is interdisciplinary. I have not thought that much as to how one goes about this. I am in partial agreement with students who want more individualization and want to design their own curriculum, in part with the realization that that doesn't work as well as we would like it to. Experimental colleges work very well for some students when they are designed by contract, but it has worked not at all for others. I could give specific examples from friends of my own children.

What I would like to put forth is that there should be a certain amount of required courses. They should be there, and the courses should be reinforced in their depth by drawing on student interest and involvement. But we should not force every student into the same mould in going through college. Here, an extremely good advisor system is best felt so that an attainment at a higher level should be expected and demanded, no matter what the subject. So I wouldn't prescribe a set curriculum, but it should contain some element of the sciences with their insights. Certainly the experience and thoughts of man must be part of the baccalaureate degree. What must be done is to rethink and plan the quality of the liberal arts. Everything called "liberal arts" does not mean, automatically, that it represents quality. At one school I know about, everyone had to take the "Courses," and the expectation was that everyone graduating was liberally educated. They packed them into the lecture halls. They had to pass very tough examinations. The trouble is, the courses were lousy. The students when finishing them said, "Thank God I'll never have to go through that again." Se we certainly don't want that kind of thing masquerading as reform.

*Isn't the answer, partially, that the students have to show the interest? Don't students themselves rebel against too much professionalism?

Of course, we had much less pressure during the sixties than colleges at an undergraduate level. Our students were goal oriented and had been in a highly competitive environment, had been a part of that "gray homogeneous mass of compulsive over-achievers"--terms I don't like, by the way. My daughter uses them with me multiple times, however.

But what we went overboard on in medical schools was requirements. We get the students in lock step, and they march along with their ankles almost chained together. If we do tests in creativity at the end of the first year of medical school, they do worse than they did at the beginning of the first year, because they have such a tremendous amount of memorization. We haven't been able to get away from that because there's no other way to know what's in the human body but to learn it. So that year is a dehumanizing experience. That's the last thing I'll think of when I'm at the end of my days and I recall the first year of medical school, the rough awakening when I had to work hard.

However, our own faculty did make one year out of the four an elective year, supervised and controlled. But it was a great improvement in the medical school curriculum. We also allow that to be spread out so that the lock step can be broken. I do wish that we had time for the students to pursue things in off years. One medical student I know did not fit the usual mould. He went to Carlton College, which is devoted to the liberal arts, and seriously studied music. We see this in a lot of our students. Many of them are interested in music and other humanities.

Finally, let me say that if there is anything that we can do from our level to support the strengths of the liberal arts and humanities, we should do it. Perhaps, we should have our national medical association in medicine communicate our feelings of importance which our people have, our deans, our faculty, about the liberal arts. Studying

31

these subjects, such as English literature, does show a balance that actually helps students get into medical school. That should be mentioned.

THE PLACE OF LAW IN
UNDERGRADUATE LIBERAL EDUCATION

Robert S. Summers

I do not propose to offer a comprehensive account of liberal education. Instead, I propose something far more modest, though some may think it still quite ambitious. I will discuss in a general way the role of one, or preferably a few, basic courses dealing appropriately with law as part of an undergraduate liberal education. In so doing, I will be telling you about something with which I have had experience. At the same time, this will enable me to bring out at least the bare essentials of my own conception of a liberal education.

Today, law is not widely taught as part of a liberal education. Professor Paul A. Freund of Harvard University has remarked that "Law is probably the most neglected phase of our culture in the liberal arts curriculum." It is commonly assumed that since law is widely offered as a specialist subject in professional law schools, it must follow that it has no content suitable for inclusion in a liberal education. But this does not follow. It is true that law can be presented solely from a technical point of view. And it is true that this is what many of our law schools do--all except such schools as Cornell, Yale and Chicago! But in my view, any subject can be presented liberally.

As Alfred North Whitehead put it, "there is not one course of study which merely gives culture and another which merely gives special knowledge. The subjects pursued for the sake of a liberal education are special subjects." Law, of course, is a special subject in Whitehead's terms. I will contend not only that it can be presented liberally, but also that it has a distinctive place in a well-structured liberal education for undergraduates.

Training of the intellect and of powers of expression are prime objectives of liberal education. The student must learn to think and to express thought. Many subjects can be taught to these ends, a course on law distinctively so. In legal materials, and especially in opinions of appellate judges, one finds unusually rich quarries of reasoning, argument, and analysis. Of course, the arguments of judges and lawyers are not always sound, but this makes them all the better grist. It will not do to object that the reasoning in court opinions is too technical in nature. I recently did a fairly elaborate study of the types of reasons that judges give in common law cases. It turns out that much judicial reasoning derives from ordinary reason-giving practices in everyday life. Judges are called upon to refine their reasons, and they make special efforts (not always successful) at articulation. It is easy to concur with Sir Francis Bacon, one of the early students of liberal education. Bacon said of the student unskilled in analysis, "Let him study the lawyer's cases."

To work at all fruitfully with law, the undergraduate must confront at least some primary source materials such as judicial opinions, regulations and statutes. Indeed, in law perhaps more than in any subject except poetry, much can depend on the meaning of a single word. To cope with law faithfully, precise and clear expression is a necessity (and cannot be mastered in a single course, but then no one claims that the essentials of a liberal education can be derived from a single course). It is hardly surprising that a lawyer, Cicero, had a large hand in founding rhetoric--one of the original liberal arts.

To provide broad perspective is also a fundamental aim of liberal education. But what is perspective? I will explore three different meanings. To understand some of the possibilities and limits of human achievement is to acquire one kind of perspective. From studies of science, the undergraduate can see that our scientific achievements would have awed the ancient Greeks. Yet the student can see, too, that much remains unknown and may even be unknowable. If it is well for the student to confront some of the possibilities and limits of human achievement in science, why not also in law? Law affects the student at least equally, and seems even more accessible to most. That we have devised a liberal and pluralistic legal order capable of governing such a vast, populous, complex, and tension-ridden society as the United States is no minor achievement. Law can help keep the peace (indeed, to that end it is indispensable). Law can help reinforce the family, preserve basic freedoms, protect ownership, secure the conditions of individual self-realization, and more. At the same time, law too has real limits. Law cannot prevent all crime. It cannot make people love each other. There are things it cannot do for interracial peace. It is not very effective at coercing belief. Like science, law is not without limits.

A second kind of perspective is more historical. Man striving to adjust to change, and to control change--these are dominant themes of recorded history. Undergraduates have always been expected to study the past as part of liberal education. Might some understanding of the law distinctively enrich this study? The forces of change in any given period seldom fail to manifest themselves in the law, a fact which should startle no one, for law, with its principles, rules, and directives, its preventive and remedial devices, and its diverse institutions and processes, is organized society's chief means of implementing policy. In addition, because the demands of predictability commit law to some forms of continuity, the case for change in and through law must be and has often been explicitly argued and recorded. The law is a force of history as well as a source of history. Law--legal institutions, structures, processes, and precepts--shape whole patterns of life in society and frequently regulate the very nature and course of change.

The student derives still another type of perspective from study of the varieties of human thought and knowledge. He or she can come to see that major branches of learning differ importantly in orientation, in structure, in modes of analysis, and in criteria of truth. Science as a subject is not to be equated with history. Law differs radically from both. But to grasp such differences, and also to see significant similarities and connections, undergraduates must immerse themselves in each of the relevant subject matters. Ultimately, they should emerge with a kind of breadth and synoptic perspective that is one mark of the liberally educated.

Aside from inculcating perspective, another basic objective of liberal education is to develop an appreciative understanding of social values and ideals. The law's special claim to inclusion here rests mainly, (but not solely) on the fact that it is the most important scene of interaction between social ends and means. The undergraduate is offered literature, philosophy, political theory, and much else, though seldom legal materials. But why not these? Law inevitably and regularly reckons with social values and ideals of highest order. In the law, as much or more is explicitly made of some social ideals than in any other branch of learning! Consider, for example, fairness. In a healthy legal order, the law insists on letting each side to a dispute be heard, and it lets only one side talk at a time. It strives to protect justified expectations, ever a demand of fairness. And it purports to decide like cases in like manner, often a complex affair. Consider next the ideal of rationality. The progressive reduction of arbitrariness in human relations ought always to be one of the law's chief concerns. By duty, appellate judges give reasons for what they decide, and they frequently require administrative and other officials to justify their actions. In fact, some social values and ideals cannot be adequately appreciated without an exposure to law, for they are quasi-legal in nature. This is true, for instance, of official impartiality and of procedural due process. Thus we tend to think of official hearings as technical matters designed solely as means of providing the decision maker with more evidence and argument to achieve a better result. This is much too narrow a view. There are "process values" at work here, including fairness and participation. These are important in their own right, independently of outcome.

Moreover, some values, though not quasi-legal, depend partly for their realization upon appropriate forms of legal ordering. Freedom from wrongful detention by the state is an important example, and it is secured partly by the ancient writ of habeas corpus. Indeed, it would be hard to know just what such freedom means apart from a legal procedure in the nature of habeas corpus. Of course, this is not to say either that law is the only guarantor of freedom, or that wherever there is law there is always freedom.

In addition, legal materials have distinctive value as a medium in which and through which a sensitive and appreciative understanding of social values and ideals may be taught. The specific and concrete is inherently more meaningful than the general and abstract. Much law is concerned with actual cases out of which specific and concrete embodiments of general values and ideals graphically protrude. Consider the values associated with free expression. The study of a case in which a court holds unconstitutional an ordinance in the name of which police have stopped a man from advocating his political views can prove far more meaningful to the student than reading hundreds of pages of general and abstract textual discussion of free speech.

But it is not just because of their concreteness and specificity that well-selected legal materials may have unique value as a teaching medium. They readily evoke empathy. Students will identify with one side in a law case and thus absorb themselves in active thought about the relevant values and ideals and their bearing on the particular facts.

Furthermore, in a law case, the judge must sometimes make a hard choice between values and ideals which, in the particular circumstances, have come into conflict. The conflict may be between the high demands of public order on the one hand and free expression on the other. I believe that the undergraduate who vicariously re-enacts such choices, carefully evaluating the justifications judges have given for them, will appreciate the nature of the values and ideals at stake better than if he or she were to read treatises on free speech.

Certain general truths of social life accumulated from the collective experience of mankind also comprise a part of undergraduate liberal education. For example, one may cite certain truths of experience about human nature. That political power tends to corrupt, and absolute political power tends to corrupt absolutely, is familiar enough. More often, when government goes awry, officials are simply misguided in some way. History underscores these truths. What of the law? Actually, these truths are among the very justifications for having law itself--for having a government "of laws and not of men." In a legal system worthy of the title, legal methods of surveillance are provided in order to keep the officialdom within bounds. Hence we have such devices as appeals, legislative oversight, and, latterly, the office of ombudsman. As David Hume put it, "A constitution is only so far good as it provides a remedy for maladministration.

In addition to the foregoing, liberal education should inspire its students. To this, law too might contribute. Of course, law can be instructive both negatively and positively. For example, the legal facets of Watergate, (and other "gates") have communicated a great deal about what we ought not to strive for. But more positive and less dramatic inspiration is possible, too. Well designed legal processes publicly display respect for truth: the application of law depends intrinsically on findings of fact. Law may inspire sensitivity to encroachments upon the ideals with which it reckons. The professional accomplishments of the great men and women of the law may also have inspirational value.

A good liberal education also helps to prepare the student for organized life in society. It therefore must not neglect the theory and practice of democracy. Merely because this has practical value, it hardly follows that it is not suitable for liberal education. But where does the law come in? In a democracy, the citizenry has ultimate responsibility for the law. This is not a responsibility to be discharged by citizens who have only the vaguest notion of law, or, indeed, have positive misconceptions of it. Yet I regularly encounter citizens who believe one or more of the following: That law is necessarily and essentially coercive and restrictive, rather than consensual and facilitative; that legal procedures are mere technicalities, and do not in themselves protect significant process values; that law consists exclusively of hard and fast rules always to be applied strictly according to their letter and never in light of their spirit; that courts may and should freely act on their own initiative to correct social ills rather than wait for disputants to bring cases to them; and that law is capable of doing anything and everything--provided that we do a good job of suiting means to ends. Citizens with these and other misconceptions of the legal system are less than qualified to have much say about it. In 1894 Woodrow Wilson emphasized that "We need laymen who understand the necessity for law and the right uses of it . . . ." This bears re-emphasis today. These are fast moving times. We are in the midst of megalopolis explosions, great technological change, environmental crises, and more. In all of these the legal system is involved in complex and countless ways. Of course, undergraduate study dealing broadly with the legal system is only a partial solution to the problem of combating fundamental misconceptions of law and its processes.

The undergraduate who studies no law at all must inevitably emerge with a truncated conception of governmental processes. For these processes may be viewed as complexes of means and ends, adjusted to each other in all sorts of ways, with the relevant means consisting mainly of various forms of law.

The law is too important to be left to the lawyers. The lawyers themselves must be watched, for they may overextend legal ideas and legal ways of doing things into spheres in which they have no place. This vice has been called "legalism." To recognize legalism in its varied manifestations, the citizen must be armed with some grasp of what law is, of how law operates, and of conditions under which law and legal modes of operation are generally effective.

Furthermore, if the law is left to lawyers and other experts we may get not only bad law but loss of democracy as well. This is not fanciful, and I cite only one dramatic and perhaps controversial example close to home. During the 1960's, our labor relations experts, most of whom were lawyers, put their heads together and engineered public employee collective bargaining laws. All of this was done in most states without anyone even pausing to reflect that laws of this nature drastically diminish local democracy, for they transfer public law making power to private labor organizations.

Problems of social ordering crop up in nearly all fields of endeavor and not just in those where the law happens to have been at work. From exposure to the law, the undergraduate may derive insights transferrable to social ordering outside the law's domains. Through law and legal materials it is possible to see, perhaps more clearly than through any other medium, such things as that general rules are a necessity, and for a variety of reasons; that we cannot, however, put all our stock in rules for they are inevitably imperfect, since men are fallible, language is inadequate, and the future is unknowable; that rules are most intelligently applied when interpreted in accordance with their spirit and purpose rather than their letter alone; that it is wise to agree upon and thus legitimize principles and procedures for resolving foreseeable disputes well in advance of occasions when they might arise; that if third parties are to be called upon to resolve disputes because of their assumed impartiality, positive steps must be taken to institutionalize this impartiality; that to require reasons for decisions is to provide safeguards against arbitrariness and guidance for the future; and that precedents (laymen often appeal to precedents) afford guidance only in subsequent situations similar in relevant respects.

Then, finally, there is the problem of respect for law. Some study of the nature and the role of law in society should foster, if not in all cases respect for law, at least a more intelligent disrespect for it when disrespect is due.

Alexis de Tocqueville, were he to return, would almost certainly be surprised to find that law has not yet achieved a place in the undergraduate curriculum in most of our universities and colleges. In the 1830's, de Tocqueville was quick to observe what continues to be true today: namely, the tendency of Americans to convert many if not most significant social questions into legal questions. Yet, in some countries where this tendency has been much less evident, law has now achieved a place of far greater prominence in the general educational system than it has in the United States. Thus in British universities such as Oxford and Cambridge, undergraduates study law as a B.A. major. While in my view this is less than ideal, still it is evidence that if I am wrong about the importance of law in good liberal education, I am in very good company indeed.

QUESTIONS

*I didn't get anything from your talk that would define what kind of liberal study would prepare students for the study of the law. What do you recommend?

When I spoke of the breadth of liberal education and the development of synoptic perspective, taking into account the ways of analysis in different fields, I was referring to some of the features of liberal education that make it ideal preparation for law.

*Is history still a primary study for law, particularly English and American history?

Yes, it is. However, I would like to see law cases themselves brought into the study of history. This would provide a more intensive understanding of certain significant historical processes.

*Isn't there a problem with the legal education of lawyers now practicing, that most of their education has been too narrow? What is the education necessary for a good lawyer, not just a technician of the law?

Our students should work with comparative law, legal history, jurisprudence, and modern legal philosophy. Now, not enough law students study these subjects, but a very much higher proportion take them at Cornell than at most other law schools. We could do a more satisfactory job of integrating liberal education and legal education. Students come to us with sixteen years of education, the last four of those, we may hope, immersed to a considerable degree in a liberally oriented curriculum. I think in law school we would do better to draw more explicitly on that previous experience, demonstrating the connections between their undergraduate years and what they are doing in law school. For example, a good lawyer is good not just at technical legal argument but also at articulating and bringing to bear ordinary substantive reasoning. Such reasoning consists of moral, political, economic and other social considerations. Law students enter law school with a good deal of ability in those very terms. We should build on this more explicitly.

I might add here that, among legal educators, one of my heroes is a man named Lon Fuller, who died in April, 1978. Fuller was one of the leading American legal philosophers. He thought law schools also have a distinctive contribution to make in preparing the liberally educated lawyer because the law schools operate at the point at which means and ends interact in social reasoning. Thus, for the student in the liberal arts curriculum only to study economic policy and the ways of developing and evaluating policy proposals, without any immersion in law, is to present a truncated view of the policy process. Policy ideas, taken alone, as they usually are in the undergraduate curriculum, represent efforts to think about ends in abstraction from means. Fuller once quoted from the economist, Paul Samuelson, some very interesting passages in which Samuelson says society ought to do certain things, as a matter of policy. Samuelson said that the ways in which we can do them is entirely something else. Well, Fuller argued that this separation is false, and that we have the opportunity in law school to put all this together. Continuing with the example of economics, economic policy has to be implemented through legal forms, processes, procedures, through legal methodology, with perhaps some element of managerial discretion, but still within a legal context. So we in the law schools ought to be undertaking that kind of integration. If we were to do that, we would then bring home to the student how means and ends do interact in the process of social decision making. We would bring home to the student how we may start with a policy proposal, but when we look at the available modes of implementation we may conclude that the policy must be considerably refined, modified, perhaps in some cases even abandoned. That's a dimension Fuller argued has been lacking in most liberal education. Consider the implementation of democracy as a second example. We may, in an undergraduate political theory course, read a hundred pages about the ends of democracy, but Fuller says we also ought to give the students some problems where they have to develop their powers and capacities for responsible social thought,

43

some problems where conflicts arise between the ends, means, and techniques of democracy on the one hand, and various social values on the other.

*There are several familiar treatments of law in literature, philosophy, history, the trial of Socrates, the issues in <u>Antigone</u>, and some major Supreme Court decisions in American history. Yet undergraduate faculties are not up on current traffic law or tax law --

Now it's clear you have misunderstood me. I'm not, for purposes of liberal education, interested in a course that undertakes to tell the students what the tax laws are, nor am I interested in a course that undertakes to tell the students what the burial laws are.

*Yes, but how does one bridge these differences?

I think there is scope here for distinctive contributions of law at the undergraduate level. I would like to see some legal material not only in the hands of teachers of history and literature, bringing their own distinctive perspective to bear on it, but I would also like to see the teaching of such materials in the hands of persons who have considerable jurisprudential conversancy. Jurisprudence, or legal philosophy, is itself a discipline. This is unknown not only to a great many very well educated people; it is, unfortunately, unknown in many law schools.

*If it's so important and significant, admittedly, why isn't law part of the undergraduate curriculum?

In the latter part of the nineteenth century, law was an undergraduate subject in this country just as it continues to be today at Oxford, which awards the B.A. in Jurisprudence. Toward the end of the nineteenth century in America a professionalization of legal education started taking place and the law became the province of a kind of professorial priesthood that separated itself unduly from the rest of the university. Law eventually became a graduate study, and the next thing we knew nearly all forms of instruction involving legal matters were abstracted from the liberal arts curriculum, the exceptions being constitutional law and sometimes international and business law, which are still found in some undergraduate departments. One result is that the law, like medicine, is thought of today as something technical, professional, vocational. We've also concluded that there isn't room in the undergraduate curriculum. The mistake should be rectified.

BEYOND THE MACHINE - LIBERAL EDUCATION FOR AN INFORMATION SOCIETY

Bruce E. Strasser

The concept of a "liberal education" comes from the notion that knowledge in the arts and humanities liberates one from the bounds of ignorance, thereby opening intellectual vistas as well as more possibilities for an enjoyable life. The broader the knowledge, the greater the freedom. A liberal education prepares us to understand and respond more fully and effectively to the exigencies of life, to avoid repetition of past errors and to grasp opportunities. It imparts knowledge, cultivates the intellect so that we may think and reason well, and bestows ethics for guiding us in the use of knowledge for the benefit of ourselves and our society.

While few would take issue with such laudable objectives, many disagree on how to achieve them. Some educators interpret "liberal" to mean "broad," and they load up curricula with smorgasbords of trendy and trivial electives designed to attract and entertain students, while "difficult" traditional courses in the arts and sciences go unattended. The result can be college graduates with easy degrees who have neither the basic education nor the intellectual discipline to work and live in a society that is as advanced technologically, complex, and continually changing as ours.

In these times, a liberal arts education -- one that maintains its traditional pursuit of knowledge and excellence -- is far from an anachronism or luxury. It can play a powerful role in shaping business, industry, government and the quality of life itself.

The students you are educating today are graduating into a vastly different society than in the past -- a society that has moved beyond one based on agriculture or on simple machines that transform raw materials into manufactured products -- to one which is technologically advanced and increasingly engaged in the production, processing, and distribution of information.

This evolution into an Information Society is having social and economic impacts as profound and far reaching as the industrial revolution. Already more than half the United States work force is engaged in information-related activities, or in developing and operating the vast infrastructure of telecommunications networks and computers that makes them possible.

This Information Society needs people who are knowledgeable about science and technology and who have new kinds of skills and intellectual abilities that will enable them to cope with and make the most of recent advances in information technologies. These technologies are transforming not only the way we live and work but our relationships with other people and the basic aspirations and values of our society.

Lewis Mumford pointed out, "Our capacity to go beyond the machine rests upon our power to assimilate the machine. Until we have absorbed the lessons of the mechanical realm, we cannot go further in our development towards the richly organic, the more profoundly human."

Understanding these new technologies is a prerequisite to controlling them, to make them our servants instead of our masters, to use them to enhance our lives and strengthen human values.

In short, in any technologically-advanced society, a liberal education without science is a contradiction in terms. And in a post-industrial information society, the mastery of information machines -- computers and telecommunications -- is essential and should be as much a part of a liberal

47

education as books, pencils, and blackboards were in previous ages.

The idea of science as part of a liberal education is not new. Early medieval universities included medicine along with art, law, and theology as major areas of study. After Copernicus, in 1548 astronomy became part of the curriculum.

Early seventeenth century universities offered arithmetic, geometry, and astronomy along with grammar, logic and rhetoric. The educated gentleman could aspire to learning virtually all that was known. And while the nobility educated its children in languages, literature, music and art, it did not neglect engineering for warfare and defense. Mathematics and astronomy were studied for purposes of navigation in an increasing mercantile world.

Francis Bacon considered all knowledge, including the sciences, to be the province of the educated man. He promulgated in Novum Organum the idea that learning should have a purpose beyond knowledge for its own sake. Knowledge provided power that could be used to enhance the quality of life.

Yale University's charter, written in 1701, was a little ahead of its time in stating explicitly that students should "be educated that they might be fitted for public employment both in church and civil state."

During the industrial revolution, although education in the arts and humanities was always available, colleges and universities increasingly offered professional training in specific fields such as engineering, science, medicine, business administration, and law. As the specific knowledge required for professional careers increased, there simply wasn't time (or the inclination) to provide more than a cursory look at the arts and the humanities.

C. P. Snow in 1956 lamented this specialization and warned of the consequences of the diverging cultures of science and literature.

Since then, the two cultures have further divided into many more. As more and more information is generated in all fields -- science, engineering, law, medicine, history, art, etc. -- it is impossible for a person to be fully knowledgeable in more than one or two subjects. Scholars and practitioners have had to narrow their focus. People knowledgeable in one subject have difficulty understanding people expert in other areas. Our society has become inundated with knowledge and fragmented with specialization.

This isolation within and between the arts and the sciences has generated cries to do something about it. Reintegrate education! Teach science in humanities courses and include the arts in engineering courses! Teach physicians about the law and lawyers about humanity! And at the same time remedy deficient secondary school education and teach everyone how to read and write!

That is easier said than done. There are, after all, time and money limits in any curriculum. However, information age technologies are providing some help. Computer programs and video tapes on a wide variety of subjects are available for students or post graduates who wish to educate themselves in subjects outside their major field. A liberal arts naculty could provide guidance in the selection of these electronic courses and be available to answer questions or lead informal discussion groups.

Also, intelligent and relatively inexpensive telecommunications networks are making it possible for people in all fields to manage information better, to supplement their own knowledge with information quickly retrieved from distant computer data banks, and to communicate with virtually anyone, anyplace, anytime.

What kind of education will best prepare a student for earning a livelihood in the Information Age? Certainly specialists will continue to be sought by business and industry. Communications scientists and engineers, computer scientists and operators, software programmers and program designers are needed for the management and movement of information in all forms, voice, data and images.

Although it has been said that by the year 2000 less than ten percent of the United States labor force will be directly engaged in manufacturing (the jobs will have been exported overseas!), there is a growing realization that for the nation to survive in an increasingly competitive world, its crumbling industrial infrastructure must be rebuilt. Highly-trained engineers, architects and skilled technicians and laborers will be needed to build factories and mines, steel mills and oil refineries, roads, bridges, and transportation systems. Energy shortages, environmental pollution, health and safety concerns must be addressed. The nation's security will require high-tech weapons.

Physicians, lawyers, accountants, bankers, stock brokers, teachers, managers, administrators, government officials and office workers will continue to be in demand.

What about the liberal arts? Are there no places in the Information Age for the traditional arts and humanities major?--yes, of course, in the traditional fields of education and the arts, and in the burgeoning information age industries of journalism, publishing, television and entertainment. Also, as in the past, some liberal arts majors will find their way into business and government, probably at starting salaries half that of engineering, law or business administration majors.

The difference will be that in all occupations new generations of computers, faster, smarter and less costly than before, will play a greater role.

Knowledge of computers and computer networks, what they can do, and how to use them, will be the keys to success in the business and professional world.

Actually, businesses, especially high-tech companies, have underestimated the potential value of recruits with liberal arts educations. Employees with broad educations have a wide base from which to draw ideas useful for solving problems. They may be more able than technical specialists to assimilate large amounts of information and cope with ambiguity. They may be more sympathetic to consumer needs and wishes, employee concerns, community relations, affirmative action, business ethics and politics -- all of which rarely lend themselves to technological "fixes." As businesses merge and become larger and their internal organizations become more compartmented, people with general educations can function as links between departments through which ideas from one specialty stimulate others. And they may be well suited for management, whose main functions are to stimulate, evaluate and reinforce the creative ideas and people that offer the best chance for the organization to grow and adapt in a changing environment. Of course, in a high-tech business, a manager with a liberal arts background must also acquire a thorough knowledge of the company's technology. Some training in basic science as an undergraduate will considerably facilitate this post-graduate self-education.

Some liberal arts students go on to graduate schools for professional training in the law, intending eventually to pursue careers in government. Do they realize that more than half the legislation that comes before the United States Congress and State legislatures is concerned with science or technology? At present, very few legislators and their staffs have science or engineering educations. Air and water pollution, health care, agricultural pesticides, depletion of natural resources, energy generation, transportation, communications and high-tech weaponry require some knowledge of science in order

51

to understand the issues. Wouldn't it be nice if politicians could at least separate the nontechnical from the technical aspects of an issue and know enough to seek technical advice before they take positions? An awareness of the limitations and possible detrimental effects of new technologies, and the ability to question proposals that speak only of benefits, will help considerably towards the writing of sensible laws and regulations and the conservation of public funds.

One of the tasks of a liberal arts education is to enhance a student's ability to think critically rather than act routinely and to make decisions based on good value judgments. A liberal education should produce citizens who can determine what should be done humanistically, in contrast to what engineers say can be done technically. This requires analytic ability, the willingness to observe and question, and to integrate and synthesize disparate knowledge in several fields into coherent wholes. With new technologies continually altering the spectrum of choices and problems that our society faces, and any decision likely to generate more problems and choices and the need for more decisions, this process has become very complicated.

However, with the help of computers, instantly accessible data bases and expert computer programs, liberal arts graduates with only a basic knowledge of technology can be prepared for active citizenship in the information age.

Therefore, in their role of producing an educated citizenry, liberal arts colleges should be giving their students an appreciation of, and perspective on, the technologies underlying our society.

With such knowledge they will be better able to assess new technologies and proposed projects: to ask penetrating questions and challenge dubious statements, to examine facts and conventional values critically, and to anticipate a broader range of future

52

consequences and alternatives in using or misusing the technologies.

Science and technology pervade our culture. They are among mankind's greatest intellectual achievements. Therefore, science literacy should be a legitimate aim of a liberal arts education. That means, as Jacques Barzun said, knowing enough about science and technology to appreciate what they have to offer the world. One needs not be a scientist to appreciate the beauty and significance of its accomplishments any more than one needs be a musician to appreciate music, an artist to appreciate painting, or an author to appreciate literature.

Science literacy is a hallmark of an educated person and will, it is hoped, encourage citizens to be agents of social change; that is, not only to contribute towards the continuity of our culture, but also to participate intelligently in shaping its future.

Obviously science literacy of this nature cannot be achieved by forcing liberal arts students to sit through courses in basic physics, chemistry or mathematics designed for students planning careers in science and engineering. Trying to cram specific formulae, facts and scientific principles into students already somewhat afraid of science and suspicious of technology will only increase the culture gap.

Instead, science and technology for liberal arts students should be taught as aspects of our culture that are having a profound bearing on traditional concerns of the humanities: philosophy, arts, religion, history, ethics and values, world views, etc. and how they are affecting decision making in everyday life and world affairs.

In the past decade or so, many colleges and universities have experimented with this approach with varying degrees of success. More than 120 programs and 1000 courses in 500 institutions of higher education have addressed the impact of science and technology on ethics, values, the arts, religion, humanities, economics, environment, national security, etc.

For example: the State University of New York at Stony Brook in 1978 initiated an interdisciplinary program entitled "Technology, Values and Society."

Stanford University instituted a "Values, Technology and Society" program with a year-long course entitled "Ethics and Development in a Global Environment." It investigated the problems of pollution, energy, food, waste removal, among others, and what science and technology can and cannot do to solve them.

Lehigh University had a program called "Humanities Perspective on Technology" and a strong extra-curricula program that included faculty suppers with lectures on the social aspects of technology, a lecture series funded by the Mellon Foundation that brought in outside speakers, half-day symposia on subjects such as "Science and Music," a science film series, and science news broadcast regularly on campus radio.

Massachusetts Institute of Technology experimented with a "College of Science, Technology and Society" staffed by many of its faculty members.

And long standing programs at Penn State, Rensselaer, Carnegie Mellon, and Cornell encouraged smaller colleges to try similar courses.

Whether these programs have been successful is difficult to assess. Some programs have been dropped, others have been changed, and new courses have been started. In any case, there has been some recognition of the need for science literacy among liberal arts students and some progress towards closing the gap between the humanities and the sciences.

Some liberal arts faculties (at Yale, Amherst, Middlebury, Cornell, Stanford, Johns Hopkins, to name a few) have in recent years been engaged in revising their undergraduate curricula. Some, like Harvard, moved in the direction of restoring core curriculum requirements and reinstating standards and measurements that dissipated during the student demonstrations of the 1960's.

Other faculties are still struggling to regain control over course content and curriculum design. Vestiges of the egalitarianism of the '60's, which resulted in grade inflation, in some instances abolition of grades, and the belittlement of individual merit can still be seen on some campuses. Some students still resist literacy requirements and insist on their right to pick and choose from among hundreds of courses, all presumably of equal value, and to withdraw without prejudice from those that are too demanding. Others, the so-called "me generation," rush to sign up for those courses that promise instant success on Wall Street or in business.

I encourage you to resist the political and financial pressures that tempt colleges to be all things to all students. My business colleagues and I hope you will find ways to recommit students and faculty to the search for knowledge and to the pursuit of excellence.

High-grade talent is needed in business and government in an increasingly competitive world to provide the goods and services that make life more secure and enjoyable.

Obviously, my advocating more science and computer literacy in a liberal arts curriculum is based on the benefits this will bring to business and industry. I am aware that we have responsibilities, too.

First of all, business should give more support to liberal arts schools. My former company, AT&T Bell Labs, long ago realized that its future depended on a continuing input of new employees with high-quality science and engineering educations. It helped assure this by donating money and equipment to university science and engineering departments, by instituting cooperative programs in which students and faculty work part time at the company and at the university.

AT&T also developed close relations with schools of business administration. For more than two decades it has helped black colleges with direct financial aid and by lending them employees as faculty.

Business needs to do similar things for liberal arts education. It already contributes about half a billion dollars a year to higher education. Some goes to liberal arts schools through programs in which companies match contributions given by employees to colleges of their choice. But most goes to a company's interests. It should perhaps tilt more in the direction of liberal arts.

Another thing it can do is increase efforts to recruit liberal arts graduates and make better use of them when they join our companies.

Business executives often visit campuses to talk with science, engineering and business faculty and students, not only at recruitment times. There are fewer visits to liberal arts departments.

Why is that? First of all, it's a lot easier to talk with people who have already indicated by their choice of curriculum that they want to be part of the business world. Engineers, scientists and business school students are familiar with the cultures of business and industry: they speak the same language and have similar values.

Business people, on the other hand, perceive liberal arts students as naive about business matters and condescending towards business and government.

Some students, at least in the past, displayed unwelcoming, anti-business attitudes.

This is not surprising considering that the popular media often portrays business people as greedy boors and inhumane villains. And scientists and engineers are frequently portrayed as cultural illiterates involved in their formulas and machines, totally insensitive to human values.

Actually many scientists are quite broad in their interests. Some are good musicians, writers, artists and patrons of the arts. Newton wrote poetry, as did Volta, Darwin, Maxwell, and Kelvin. Many biologists and botanists are fine artists. Pasteur at the age of 18 received a certificate in art. More recent scientists with better than average writing abilities and broad cultural outlooks include Albert Einstein, C. P. Snow, Fred Hoyle, Carl Sagan, Philip Morrison, and Isaac Asimov.

About ten years ago the Dean of the Undergraduate studies at Stanford University found that engineering and science students took a significantly greater percentage of their electives in the humanities than humanities students chose science courses.

Some businesses have recognized that after years on the job their executives may become rigid and narrow in their outlook. They have established programs for executives to return to school at selected universities for three-to-six-month "refresher" courses in the arts and humanities. Some companies encouraged executives to take courses in nearby colleges. And some regularly invite educators to address them in business meetings. So business is making some effort to close the culture gap.

Perhaps the misconceptions about the character and culture of people in business and education could be dispelled if there were more opportunities for them to meet and exchange opinions, as we have done today.

You may be interested in an experimental program that AT&T Bell Labs conducted in 1979. We invited to our New Jersey labs 30 university liberal arts students and faculty members from Boston University, Iowa State, Kent State, Northwestern University, Penn State, Princeton, Purdue, Rensselaer, Rice, Chicago University, Morris Brown, Toledo Wesleyan and Wilberforce. They visited several of our laboratories and then spent two days and evenings discussing with Bell Labs scientists and engineers the implications of the technology they saw in electronics, chemistry, lightwave communications and computers.

There was a good deal of lively discussion. Its essence can be summed up in quotes from two participants. A young Sociology and English student from Rice said: "I didn't know I had so much in common with scientists and engineers. The only way we'll find solutions to today's problems is through interdisciplinary measures."

One of our scientists, a crystallographer said, "It was refreshing to meet people from a different environment, and I found myself thinking hard about the long-term implications of new technology on society."

Bell Labs intended to continue and expand this program, but unfortunately it fell victim to the break up of the Bell System and the reallocation of company resources. Another program that opened Bell Labs' considerable archives to scholars in the field of history of science and technology has continued.

I think it is important for these kinds of interactions to take place, important for business and for students who will be assuming leadership roles in society.

I hope you feel that our meeting today has been as worthwhile as I have, and that you will continue to invite business people to your seminars.

While there may be no simple answers to the task of educating people for the Information Age, I am sure together we can identify common problems and opportunities and work towards viable solutions.

QUESTIONS

*Former U.S. Secretary of the Treasury William Simon said that business should stop giving money to institutions of higher education that show anti-business attitudes. What is your reaction to such a position?

I disagree. I am aware that some businesses in the 1960's and 70's showed their disapproval to the turmoil on campuses by reducing their contributions. They thought this would persuade colleges and the students to take a more favorable attitude to business. That's not the way to do it. And it is bad public relations. Many of those anti-business attitudes came about because the students were uninformed or misinformed. And you can't correct misinformation by withdrawing from the debate. What should have been done, and what was attempted in some instances, was to open a dialogue with the dissidents. The way to change public opinion is to provide it with facts and fair interpretations, emphasize points of mutual agreement, minimize disagreements, and show by the company's integrity and actions that its policies are in the public interest.

Even during the worst of the demonstrations, I believe hundreds of millions of dollars continued to flow to colleges, from individual businesses directly and through higher education foundations funded by business, although perhaps liberal arts departments got less in those times and this was perceived as business voting its disapproval.

*So the money given to the liberal arts is predicated on the control of ideas?

As I said, it doesn't work and shouldn't be attempted. Of course, business expects something in return for its money. The way that happens, at least in the engineering field, is for a company to give grants for research and development in areas that are likely to produce new knowledge that it can use, or potential employees. Some college deans and presidents prefer to receive unrestricted money to use where they wish. Businesses are understandably perturbed if they give money for education and see it going for a new gymnasium.

*Don't we need an exchange program between business and colleges, so that the business itself will be represented in the college environment? Is there any program like this going on at present? Among other things, colleges and universities could use their management skills.

Yes. AT&T and other companies has lent business managers to universities, usually one where there are close recruiting ties, or to nearby community colleges to help with administrative problems such as setting up a computer-based information or communications system.

AT&T Bell Laboratories has since its inception more than sixty years ago shared scientists and engineers on a part time basis with universities such as Columbia, Stanford, Princeton, MIT, Caltech, etc. Often business executives upon retirement become teachers in universities.

And for many years, AT&T has provided executives as full time faculty for black colleges, and has given summer or sabbatical jobs to college faculty members. All involved -- students, teachers, colleges and the company--apparently think it is worthwhile.

*What parts of the liberal arts education would you emphasize to help people in the future deal with change and adaptation? Should there be specific courses in such subjects?

The study of history can reveal how people have adapted or failed to adapt to changes in the past. And over the years man has evolved a powerful methodology for understanding his environment. It involves carefully observing the situation and analyzing why and how it is occurring. If he can understand the why and the how, he can perhaps devise ways to cope with it and even turn it to his advantage. It is called the scientific method and it works in non-scientific fields, too.

If you could teach your students this process -- how to analyze situations and synthesize information, and come up with innovative ideas, in a variety of fields -- they might become agents of change rather than victims of it.

*What kinds of courses does Bell Labs encourage its employees to take, purely technical and scientific subjects?

Employees can take liberal arts courses, and business courses as well as science and engineering if they are credits towards a degree. Some courses are taught within the company; others are offered in nearby colleges and universities. Tuition and books are paid for by the company as long as students earn acceptable grades. In technical areas, a requisite for continuing employment is a Master's Degree.

*What do you think of the specialization of departments in colleges and universities. There is little communication between disciplines.

There is nothing wrong with specialization. It's needed in order to probe the depths of a subject, encourage excellence and to expand its frontiers. But as you imply, communications between specialties is desirable. In fact, coupling between disciplines often fosters innovations and advances. That's true in companies too.

Barriers between departments can be lowered by exchanging people temporarily or permanently, and by engaging in interdisciplinary projects. Both do wonders for broadening people and renewing enthusiasm. Similarly, exchanges of people and ideas between industry and education would be mutually beneficial.

*What about the fears concerning the computer?

Fear of computers is an ailment of mostly middle-aged people. Today, children aren't afraid. They can't wait to get their hands on a computer, some just to play games. Nevertheless, once they become familiar with it, it's an easy step to making practical use of a computer.

There are some legitimate concerns about computers: the threat to privacy and civil liberties, new joblessness, the concentration of information and power in rich technologically-advanced nations, failure or misuse of computer systems that might trigger massive economic and social disruptions. All of these issues and more are prime topics for study by liberal arts educators in courses on the impact of science and technology on society.

*Weren't some of the educational charges of the sixties needed? Your comments about the sixties were quite negative.

I didn't mean to be. When students protested against the traditional curricula they may have had legitimate gripes. After all, students are your customers and they are paying for their education. If they think their courses are not relevant they should be listened to. (Recently Stanford University responded to a similar, though less violent criticism of its Western Culture course.) What I and many of my business colleagues lamented were the inflation of grades and egos and the rejection of standards and competitive measurement. When some of the 60's students were employed and their supervisors attempted to give them performance evaluations that would determine their salaries, both were shocked. The students were unaccustomed to criticism. They could not accept that they were less than A plus employees. And some felt that their boss's opinion was no more valid than their own.

If you want to prepare your students for life and for the work environment, you would do well to hold them to high standards and tell them honestly how they are doing, even if it bruises their egos.

THE LIBERAL STUDIES AND
INSTITUTIONAL EXCELLENCE:

A Case History

Carey W. Brush

While writing a college history, I noticed a direct relationship between the intellectual atmosphere of the campus and the prominence of liberal studies in the curriculum. It is this relationship which I wish to examine today.

What, you may ask, are the liberal studies, or, if you prefer, the liberal arts? In ancient Greece, the liberal arts were those studies necessary to prepare free men for political life. In an attempt to balance physical with mental culture, letters with mathematics, and aesthetic with moral training, Greek education included, on the elementary level, grammar, drawing, music, and gymnastics, and, on the advanced level, mathematics, astronomy, rhetoric, philosophy, and dialectic, or, as we know it today, logic. In outlining his concept of the ideal education for future leaders of the state, Plato stressed arithmetic, geometry, and astronomy, but reserved the preeminent position for dialectic.

Although Plato said very little about education for the masses, his famous pupil, Aristotle, distinguished between liberal education designed to prepare the aristocracy for citizenship, and vocational education designed to fit the lower classes for an occupation. Shorn of the reference of class structure, this distinction continues to be descriptive of our system of higher education.

With some modifications, the Romans adopted and transmitted Greek ideas on liberal education. In the first century B.C., Marcus Varro defined the liberal arts as grammar, rhetoric, logic, arithmetic, geometry, astronomy, music, architecture, and medicine; but most Roman scholars spoke of the liberal arts as indefinite in number until the late fourth century A.D. At that time, Martianus Capella wrote an allegorical story entitled The Marriage of Mercury and Philology in which the seven bridesmaids represented the liberal arts of Varro minus medicine and architecture. Thus the knowledge which was basic to a liberal education had been systematized and condensed into seven disciplines largely literary and mathematical in content.

In the sixth century, Cassiodorus, a retired Roman statesman and founder of a monastic order, discovered, in the scriptures, justification for the seven liberal arts as the basis of theological study. Shortly thereafter, Isidore, Biship of Seville, used the terms trivium for the three elementary disciplines of grammar, rhetoric, and logic, and quadrivium for the higher disciplines of arithmetic, geometry, astronomy, and music.

After the fall of Rome, the liberal arts survived mainly in the monastic orders, but with an orientation quite different from their Greek origins. One authority writes:

> The spirit of Christian asceticism opposed four central features of Greek thought in liberal education: the cult of the body, intellectual and aesthetic culture, the political concept of education for service to the state, and the disparagement of manual labor.

By the time of the Renaissance, the old liberal education had become so exclusively the province of the clergy, that it was largely professional in nature. When liberal learning revived, it did so within the social milieu of the nobles and burghers of the free cities of Europe. Instead of other-worldly concerns, the new education concentrated on the study of man and his society, and the term "citizen" returned to honored usage.

65

With the humanists of the Renaissance believing that the Latin and Greek classics were the best sources for the study of human nature, grammar, which is actually language and literature in their broadest sense, became the queen of the liberal arts. In the ensuing centuries, the vernacular languages challenged the dominant position of Latin and Greek; the natural sciences contended for a place in the curriculum; and the social sciences offered new approaches to the study of man and his institutions. Thus by the end of the nineteenth century, the old concept of the liberal studies as consisting mainly of letters and mathematics had been broadened to include the natural and the social sciences. Now, instead of referring to the seven liberal arts, we speak of four major divisions of learning -- humanities, mathematics, natural sciences, and social sciences.

While the content of the liberal studies has expanded, the purpose of a liberal education remains relatively unchanged -- to prepare individuals to live the good life and to be responsible citizens. As Aristotle separated liberal education from vocational or professional studies, so the faculty of the University of Pennsylvania in 1829 agreed that liberal education "is not designed...to qualify the student in a special manner for any particular profession or pursuit...but to aid in the development of all his faculties in their just proportions; and by discipline and instruction, to furnish him with those general qualifications, which are useful and ornamental in every profession...."

A few years later, John Stuart Mill in his inaugural address as Rector of St. Andrews University in Scotland affirmed the necessity for a good liberal education before beginning professional studies. He said:

> Men are men before they
> are lawyers or physicians or
> manufacturers; and if you make
> them capable and sensible men,

they will make themselves
capable and sensible lawyers or
physicians.

More recently A. Whitney Griswold in his
inaugural address as President of Yale University
declared that the fundamental purpose of the liberal
studies "lies not in their specific content, but in
their stimulus to the individual student's powers of
reason, judgment, and imagination."

Although there is no consensus today on the
specific content which should be included in a
college undergraduate program of liberal education,
most educators recognize that any subject can be
taught liberally or illiberally -- a truth recognized
by Aristotle. A former Dean of Yale College, William
DeVane, contends that a subject is taught liberally in
direct proportion to the historical perspectives and
philosophical implications introduced. Alfred North
Whitehead in his famous essay "The Aims of Education"
warned that it is important to teach a few studies
thoroughly and imaginatively, and eliminate that
"fatal disconnection of subjects" which is the
antithesis of liberal education.

Since a liberal education traditionally connotes
a breadth of experience, there is general agreement
among educators that a student should have some
formal course work in each of the four major
divisions of learning. It is for this reason that we
often require undergraduates to study some subjects
in which they seemingly have little interest or
aptitude, and not because we agree with Mr. Dooley,
the famous American humorist of a half century ago,
who said, "It makes no difference what you teach a
boy so long as he don't like it."

In summary, a liberal education consists of
those disciplines which if studied properly will
develop that intellect which John Henry Newman
described as

...one which takes a connected
view of old and new, past and
present, far and near, and which
has an insight into the influence
of all these one to another;
without which there is no
whole, and no center. It
possesses the knowledge, not
only of things, but also of their
mutual and true relations:
knowledge, not merely considered
as acquirement, but as philosophy.

At the time when the state college in Oneonta
first opened in September 1889, professional education
as a field of study was in its infant stage. The
curriculum consisted mainly of liberal studies with
additional courses in general methods, school law,
and the history of education, together with a
practice teaching experience which was similar to a
craft apprenticeship. Since most of the students
were not high school graduates, they entered the
classical course which in four years gave them both
a high school diploma and a teaching certificate.
Note the similarity of that early curriculum to the
Greek and humanist ideas of a liberal education. It
included algebra, geometry, rhetoric, literature,
astronomy and other sciences, at least three years of
Latin, and at least three years of another language
chosen from Greek, French, or German.

From 1899 to 1905, this was the curriculum
which set the tone for campus life. The principal,
James Milne, was a scholar recognized for his
brilliance throughout the United States. To teach
under him came a band of scholars who enjoyed
distinction in their respective fields of learning.
Many of their students went on to complete
baccalaureate degrees at the leading colleges and
universities in the East, including Harvard, Yale,
Princeton, Amherst, Radcliffe, and Vassar. One of
them played a leading role in the development of
sonar, the submarine detection system; another
recently retired as a professor of chemistry at the

Massachusetts Institute of Technology and served as
a consultant to the Atomic Energy Commission; a
third became one of the country's leading
mathematicians; others had distinguished careers in the
worlds of law, medicine, business, and letters.

While I am not prepared to say that every
instructor approached his subject in the true liberal
spirit, I believe that most did. I can say unequivocally
that the spirit of liberal education permeated every
aspect of campus life, even though the academic
level of work was more nearly comparable to a
present-day preparatory school or junior college than
to a full-fledged collegiate institution.

The extra-curricular program concerned itself
mainly with music, drama, sports, argumentation, and
debate -- activities which enjoyed a high degree of
popularity in ancient Greece. Some of today's social
sororities began as literary societies during that
golden age. At their meetings, the members
discussed books and writers, frequently with invited
faculty members serving as speakers, discussion
leaders, or consultants. Often, in the evenings--
even on Saturday evenings -- faculty members
lectured on special topics from literature, philosophy,
and history. The student paper, The Oneontan, was
a quality product, and its staff exchanged with many
of the leading college papers including The Wellesley
Prelude, The Hamilton Review, and The Chicago
University News.

Almost overnight this picture changed.
Effective in 1905, a new two-year curriculum
substituted professionalized subject matter for the
liberal studies. Professionalized subject matter
consisted of a review of the common branch subjects
of the elementary schools, together with methods of
teaching them. Although a high school diploma
became a requirement for admission, the level of
academic work actually declined.

The result was disastrous. One by one the
scholarly professors of the early period died, retired,

or moved on to more challenging academic positions. The male students who had played a significant role in the intellectual life of the early period deserted the campus, and by 1910, scarcely a single man remained in the student body. The literary societies began the metamorphosis into social sororities, and the quality of The Oneontan began the slow decline which ended in oblivion by the early 1920's.

Although many school authorities soon realized what had happened, there was no change until 1922 when the state mandated a three-year program. In effect the additional year of work was in the liberal studies, but it was not always of genuine college quality. However, a growing concern for scholarship resulted in the organization of the college's first honor society, Sigma Pi Sigma, in 1929. At the same time, the Student League Board recommended the establishment of a quality-point system and academic eligibility standards for extra-curricular activities.

Because of a surplus of teachers during the great depression of the 1930's, the normal school staff was able to raise admission standards, improve the quality of the liberal studies courses, and upgrade the professional sequence. By 1935, about 60 percent of the required course work was in the liberal studies. Partly because of economic conditions in the nation, male students once more became significant in campus life, and the extra-curricular program expanded to include clubs in art, philosophy, French, mathematics, science, dramatics, and international relations.

Since 1942 the College has been a full-fledged, four-year, degree-granting institution. During this period, the place of the liberal studies in the curriculum has become more secure.

The impact of this development on other aspects of the College program is self-evident. The faculty now consists of many able scholars and creative artists who have opened new vistas to the student body not only in classes, but also through participation in lecture series, panel discussions, and symposia. Although faculty members may sometimes criticize the quality of student extra-curricular activities, there are now proportionally more student organizations concerned with ideas than at any time in the last half century. Not since the Milne period has the intellectual dialogue reached such a high level on this campus.

The lesson of our history is clear. Only when the liberal studies have enjoyed a dominant position in the curriculum has this institution -- normal school and college -- been academically respectable. During the decades when professionalized subject matter reigned supreme, the normal school was little better than a trade school. I do not foresee a return to the practices of those unfortunate days-- the trend is all in the other direction -- but as an historian I am conscious of the cyclical nature of many human events. As we chart our future course, let us remember the dictum of Santayana that "those who do not remember the past are condemned to relive it."

ON BEHALF OF THE HUMANITIES

A. Bartlett Giamatti

Of all the areas in colleges and universities that will feel the assaults of inflation, the shrinking numbers of students, the devastated job market, and particularly the growing vocationalism of the young, the humanities will be hardest hit. Yet if one speaks of the values, the value of a liberal education, the humanities ought to be central to the conversation. My concerns are for the continuing, vital existence of the humanities.

I conceive of the humanities as those areas of inquiry that are language, or better, word-centered, and I conceive of the radical humanist activity, therefore, as revolving around the interpretation of a text. My logocentricity is part of an old, relatively unphilosophical, fundamentally philological tradition. It sees language as the bearer of tradition, believes words give first principles and last things, and therefore believes that if etymology and eschatology will finally converge to clarify the life of an individual or an institution or a people, it will be because texts and the varieties of interpretation are vital concerns to that individual or institution or people. "Connexa sunt studia humanitatis," said Coluccio Salutati at the end of the fourteenth century. He was talking about the crucial role of grammar in the divine scheme of things. "Humane studies are connected to each other; religious studies (studia divinitatis) are also bound each to each; it is impossible to acquire a complete knowledge of the one science without the other." If the humanist perspective sees how things secular and sacred are connected among themselves, it sees that connection through the ligatures of language. And it is the tradition of seeing from various vantage points, the

72

principle of perspective and hence of multiple perspectives, that the humanities want to keep alive, and well.

That is my bias, which no one is obliged to share or even approve. But it is beneath what follows--which is a sense that in the last decade, incoherence has often been institutionalized; that most curricula (in high school and beyond) are no better structured than many student papers; that where requirements were replaced by guidelines, those guidelines are so lacking in force they could not guide a vulture to month-old carrion, much less anyone to self-education. It is my sense that, in general, we still tend to apply solutions of the Sixties to problems of the Seventies and Eighties-- and that those solutions do not necessarily work.

The structures and the habits of mind of a period that was expansionist, federally-supported and student oriented; of a time when faith in the college of university mission as aimed at social action was at its most intense; of a time when it was easier than ever before to assert that academic work ought to be in many ways a form of social work--the specific attitudes of that period are in some places still being asserted and assumed when those days are gone. Demographic projections now point to a dramatic lessening in numbers of college-age students in the next decade. What was several years ago characterized as a continuing crisis in financing higher education will not slacken. Faculties are becoming increasingly tenure-heavy because of legislation raising retirement ages and because there are fewer new jobs. There will be--most dangerous trend of all--less need for young faculty.

The mood, indeed all the imperatives, now point to contraction, self-sufficiency, a deepening of the pressure on faculty. Those pressures come and will continue to come most insistently from two quarters: from legislative/administrative cost benefit analysis and productivity studies, and from the increasing migration of students toward more immediately

73

"practical" and vocationally oriented subjects. Thus the humanities feel and will continue to feel this double squeeze--to justify what they do and to give others skills they can "use"--more acutely than any other segment of the university world.

It will be a hard time. While it will be true, it will not be enough to advert to the dignity of man, the connectedness among things; the way the humanities prepare for life and sharpen critical judgement, and give a keener appreciation of experience; how they express, and teach us to express, the highest values we can live by; or the way they are valuable in and of themselves. The reason this will not do is that under pressure humanists, as well as others, did not really seem to believe it. Ten to twelve years ago, it was in many places the humanists, not the hard scientists or social scientists, but the humanists, or at least people who taught in humanities departments, who wrote the guidelines that displaced the requirements for a B.A., who eloquently undermined the writing and the foreign language requirements, who instituted the grading reforms that, some would argue, did nothing to discourage other pressures that were inflating grades. You can call what happened then a new spirit of freedom; you can call it a "vocational crisis;" you can call it anything you want. The fact remains that the humanists, self-proclaimed as central and vital links to all of experience, displaced themselves, said they were not necessary to an ordered existence, even when that existence was only under-graduate education, much less society's stream of life. And in seeming to will themselves to the periphery, humanists made themselves in subsequent hard financial times perilously vulnerable.

Early in May of 1977 the faculty at a major state university in New England voted overwhelmingly for the removal of the President and the Provost, the cause for that series of votes being a plan presented by the Provost to cut a number of faculty positions and to excise two departments--Asian Studies and Slavic Languages. The language departments tend to be the first to go. The more remote, geographically, the sooner they feel the sword. When we come to European languages, it is always a nice question whether Portuguese or Italian will precede Classics when the cuts are imposed. It is an extraordinarily melancholy sight, the devastation of foreign languages in this country--the sliding enrollments and smaller and smaller numbers of faculty involuntarily justifying the analyses that proceed by the numbers. The demise of foreign languages is part of a larger assault on literacy, part of a larger decline in the capacity to handle any language at all. It is, I believe, a fact that in the last fifteen years, certainly the last ten, any American college student who knew anything about the dynamics of English--its struts and cables, its soaring spans, the way it holds together and works-- knew it by analogy from the grammar of a foreign language. (It is true, the old cliche', that says a foreign language necessarily deepens one's grasp of one's native language. And what is true about language tends to be true of culture). All the general worry about students' capacity to structure and to express their thoughts in English must include the current sorry situation with foreign languages.

But what do we expect? When most college faculties in this country will neither require for admission nor for graduation the knowledge of a foreign language, why should hard-pressed administrations think languages are crucial? If humanities faculties do not assert the mutual dependence and reliance of the various parts, then the parts, or some parts, will disappear. No one will articulate a coherent and useful view of the humanities if the humanists will not or cannot. And if the humanists do not, then what was threatened at that university I referred to, a situation where at the end of the twentieth century a student would not be able to study Russian or Chinese, or know people who were studying them, or be able to study them in translation from people who know the original, will be more and more the norm.

These remarks on foreign languages, whose plight is visible and whose position is central to the humanities, ought to be understood as including the arts, whose plight is not so visible but whose position within the humanities is no less central. These pursuits, music, theater, painting, sculpture, architecture, each with its won sign system or "language" and its own "texts," are very much a part of my view of the humanities. Here the values we think of as humanistic are given, by a private act of the imagination, public expression and exposure. The arts are particularly vulnerable, especially in institutions without professional schools of music or art or drama or architecture to act as buffers or lobbyists. These areas are vulnerable because their faculties, either performers or practitioners, often are not seen to have the clout they should have in "academic" circles; because while many students are drawn to the arts, many majors are not, and the numbers are low; and most fundamentally, because the arts are still viewed in many quarters, within the Academy and without, as accidental, not essential; as ornamental, as something vaguely suspect, faintly interesting and often useless, like exotic foreign languages. Again, unless humanities faculties and those sympathetic to them are willing and able to assert that the so-called creative or performing arts are as much a part of the way civilized life is ordered and given meaning as anything else is, then those pursuits may be hit and hit again. And so, eventually, will the allied faculties of musicology and the history of art, particularly at the graduate level, for the historical investigation of aesthetic objects is not especially valued where the aesthetic process has no real existence. We must not encourage such a view or appear to be unconcerned about its implications.

You may have noticed I refer in my remarks to humanities faculties, not humanities departments. Departments are often the bane as well as the prop of academic existence. We complain about them but we regard them as indispensable. You know we have been willing to vote to abolish grades, requirements, poverty, and war, but never departments. And yet I think that just as one cannot be captive, in order to survive, of attitudes of the recent past, so one cannot be captive of the administrative structures of the dimmer or dimmest past.

Departments were not brought down graven in stone. And no one wants, nor should one allow administrators, to define departments as if they were necessarily identical with areas of intellectual inquiry; or to regard areas of intellectual inquiry as if they were necessarily definable as departments. The ways people really think, teach and especially do research are not defined solely by departments and never have been. Of course, departments are necessary for bureaucratic and organizational purposes; of course, they serve to indicate larger zones of concern and common interest, but they must be shaped and perhaps reconceived. Departments must be administered, but not as if they were sacraments.

Humanities departments must be thought of as forces in a field rather than feudal baronies. And the faculties that inhabit these departments must be willing to assert new administrative patterns, patterns that more nearly reflect the teaching and research interests of faculties and the needs and desires of undergraduate and graduate students, than the present rigid, often arbitrary boundaries do. New administrative arrangements should not be allowed to grow like toadstools after summer rain-- there has to be a vital legitimate teaching interest to justify a new cluster or association of colleagues. But I am less worried about humanities departments undergoing rapid change than I am about seeing them atrophy and because they cannot change in a time of vocational pressure, begin to wither away. My theme is simple: academic humanists must be flexible and choose to assert themselves, even if that means consolidation of resources, even if that means changing comfortable administrative structures, before choices are forced on them, or, worse, before the power to choose is denied. If humanities faculties face their

77

responsibilities and take the lead, they will be able to change and grapple with their futures. Otherwise, hard-pressed administrations may think they must lead by invoking some principle of pseudo-equity (Everything is as Valuable as Everything Else) and slashing across the board.

What do I mean by new administrative patterns that better reflect how things are done? Simply, to revert to an earlier example, that larger language departments make common cause with smaller ones, instead of viewing everyone else as competition. To the extent it is feasible, language departments might begin to explore linguistics and its insights so that some levels and kinds of language teaching might be done in common through common techniques, rather than always by each department on its own. At the very least, some training in common procedures might be given to the graduate students who do the great bulk of undergraduate language instruction everywhere.

I am talking about literature departments pooling resources, which means teaching faculties and traditions, not to teach "comparative literature" but to teach "literature." I mean organizing faculty members and courses by definable historical periods, rather than only by languages or thematic divisions--I mean also teaching in Classical Studies or Medieval Studies or Renaissance or Enlightenment or Modern Studies or by cultural areas, like American or Afro-American Studies, and teaching and studying the art, history, literature, history of science, philosophy, religious thought of this grouping, rather than assuming each "discipline" or "subject" is forever encased in the plastic bags of the departments. We must bring together the way faculties are organized and the way they teach and think.

I am finally thinking of humanities area programs--of placing, again, a language that has or will have a hard time by itself, alone, in the context of the philosophy and history and literature and art history of that language. Organize an area that way

78

and suddenly languages like the Slavic ones or German or Italian, or any number of others, look very different. Strong Classics departments which teach history, philosophy, archeology, art, literature, numismatics and papyrology as well as the Greek and Latin languages, have always been area programs. Strong Classics departments have always been those fields of force that I would like to see us at least begin to explore as models. And these models might then be better able to explore those ways of affiliating with, and thus supporting and drawing support from, the social sciences. The insights of sociology and anthropology, of political and economic thought, of psychoanalysis are part of the way we think and teach and write. Let the curriculum follow the mind, not restrain it.

I think the humanities are definable by the kinds of materials they use; I think the humanists share common interpretive modes and angles of vision; I think connections, in innumerable ways, characterize our materials and our methods. I think common values, about humane order, a decent rationality, a spacious and civilizing flexibility, inform those materials and methods. I believe the humanities bear a tradition that is a spirit as well as a collection of texts and ways of seeing.

Humanities faculties must assert themselves. They must assert those affiliations, those common connections each to each, and assert them intellectually and administratively, in theory and in practice. If those who conceive of themselves as humanists--and they are not only academic people but all who believe in a shared core of values held by educated people through language--do not speak for themselves, no one else can or will.

DISCUSSION

Moderator: We're at the final session. Each of our speakers will have an opportunity to add to his original remarks or perhaps to respond to something that was said by one of the other speakers or someone in the audience. Professor Smith does have a plane to catch, so I will offer him the first opportunity to speak.

John Smith: A couple of points. I was struck by what seems to me to be the measure of agreement among us on common themes and topics. I take that seriously. We came from different areas, from different backgrounds, but we have had a great many perceptions in common. And unlike those who think truth comes out only as a result of conflict, I'm inclined to believe that that kind of consensus, if you ever can get it, is worth something. I say that even today when so many people have the idea that if any two people agree, then both of them must be wrong because one learned from the other.

Now, just one word about Mr. Strasser's comments. I think it's very good what he says about citizens recognizing that they are going to be non-scientists, though I have to recognize they're also going to be non-philosophers. So I have to talk as much to non-philosophers as scientists talk to non-scientists. But people in the sciences themselves also could be a little less puristic. I'm trying to put it in a friendly way, about having to teach the "unwashed," who are not going to go "into the field." I think the usual argument is that it's all so hard, it's all so arcane, it takes so long that unless we have them from two days after they were born we'll never be able to develop what we have to develop. Well, there is a sense in which this could be said of every professional subject.

On the matter of interdisciplinary courses, I wasn't arguing that we should turn the whole thing into that, by any matter of means. What I mainly see the interdisciplinary course as doing, in addition

80

to reintegrating, reconnecting fields that have been divided, is to present material where we can no longer expect that one individual will have really sufficient knowledge and grasp the intricate topic. So that, for example, one of the reasons that I'm not pressing further for the course in bio-medical ethics is that I haven't got the time to go as far as I should. I've been invited to do it but unfortunately can't, to be an intern for a year at the Georgetown Institute where I would have some better understanding, let's say, of some of the medical procedures involved. So if some questions are raised about life support systems I would have to really know what the physician does in terms of experimentation on human beings. What are some of the procedures? What does he actually do? The absence of that kind of knowledge on my part is a handicap. I have to go to another discipline for insight.

Robert Summers: Well, there are two further things I would add. It occurred to me when I was very nearly finished with the preparation of my talk that I'd left out something of very great importance, the significance of imagination. That's surely a fundamental ingredient in the liberally educated intellect, and I do think that we're now coming to know a great deal more about it than we once did.

The great lawyer, the great judge, is a person of remarkable imagination, with capacity to imagine alternatives, consequences, capacity to imagine an apt example, counter-example, illustration, to imagine varieties of alternative interpretations of an authoritative text. So if I were to draw up a list of intellectual qualities to be stressed in the course of liberal education, surely I would not want to omit the faculty of imagination.

Now, one further thing we haven't discussed is the importance of a common experience. And that's something, I hope, we might come back to at some point this afternoon. My final remark is that I too have been very much struck by the very great deal of agreement that I perceive here. It is really quite striking.

Richard Schmidt: One of the avenues I was going to develop, which I didn't use, concerned decision making and priorities in rationing. It's a very troublesome thing which needs emphasis and, of course, needs a decision--not of an individual or of one group in society--but of the entire group. It is quite clear that we in health care are now in the state of rationing because of economic considerations. We're doing this rather poorly. One has to do with the kidney disease program which was selected out of all others and put under the Medicare reimbursement irrespective of age. As we look forward to what this is going to cost in the future, the amounts are very large. I think it is now costing four billion dollars a year, just for this one group of people, in terms of dialysis and organ transplantation. We need to consider what we're going to do with the coronary bi-pass surgery which is now using one percent of the total health care dollar expended in the United States. In other words a lot more than a billion dollars a year is spent on a procedure which we have not yet agreed is worthwhile in terms of anything other than relieving pain as opposed to actually arresting the progress of the basic disease. I was proceeding along the line of bringing the other disciplines into decision making and perhaps beginning with the design of courses in college that prepare people for lives in society to participate in these types of decision. We're now at the point where decisions of this nature are made by local bodies of which the majority are consumers--health services, agencies, and boards.

But how are we to get the conversation among these disciplines to prepare out students, who are going to be consumers, to deal with these broad ethical problems? I'm using only the model of medicine.

Bruce Strasser: I just want to say that we must try and not underexpect. Encourage college faculty to regain control of standards and to gain control of what the curriculum of the college should be before it gives someone a degree, that the responsibility for the development of a person is the individual, and if we can instill that fact in students, that they are responsible for their own education and continuing development. We should make their standards high so that they will not underexpect what we expect of them. I think that will go a long way toward creating people who will have success in business and in life.

*In the illustration that you gave about the National Humanities Institute, you mentioned several interdisciplinary projects that the persons working there had undertaken. They were in the nature of research projects. Trying to look at the liberal education in the curriculum, while there may be some room for independent undergraduate or individual undergraduate research, it's necessarily limited. Do you think that that type of integrative bringing together of various disciplines in a particular topic can be handled in the classroom?

John Smith: Well, I do certainly believe this can be done. I feel about it a little bit like the person who, when asked whether he believed in infant Baptism, said "Believe it? Why I've seen it." Now let me correct one misapprehension, at least I think it's that. To distinguish between the context in which these people develop these syllabuses which were intended for courses in the undergraduate college, and the kind of thing they were doing in the Institute itself: I'm not suggesting that one should reproduce that type of situation inside the undergraduate college. No, but I'm saying I see the kind of thing happen even in the developing of the courses, and the syllabuses involve situations where the material to be covered really requires the cooperation of a joint attack on the subject. And I'm not proposing to dissolve the whole curriculum to do that. But one thing seems to be fairly clear on the basis of courses that have already been instituted across this country along those patterns; they give living examples inside of a college of the kind of thing that can happen when we have three people, let us say, working together on a topic, because it gives an indication that these subjects themselves are refracted rays of an experience which doesn't come by subject matter, but as we know, comes whole.

Again I'd like to repeat I don't propose the transformation of the whole curriculum into that form though I do think people in the humanities should take a page out of the books of the sciences where people learn that cooperative endeavor is the essence of the process of learning and discovery. If I didn't remember to mention it yesterday, my favorite example of this was said by Schopenhauer a long time ago. He said: You know philosophers always claim that they're in the pursuit of truth. What a remarkable thing it is how little of it they find in the books of their colleagues.

*What courses, if any, should all students have to take? Would you recommend specific liberal arts requirements?

John Smith: What is obvious is that we all weigh in, first, as human beings, prior to any of the roles, specialties, professions in which we later engage. I'm obviously going to have to face certain moral dilemma that I will not get through my life without attempting to resolve. Whereas it's quite likely that I'll be able to get along without an intimate knowledge of Persian art. Now there may be a sense in which I ought to be up on that, but the fact of the matter is that there are certain structural elements of human existence in which we all participate. To that extent, I should emphasize courses dealing with individual responsibility, concern, and the recognition of the reality of other persons.

Robert Summers: Well, the first thing I would say is, in essence, a reaffirmation of what John

Smith has just said: there are certain really fundamental values, dignity, fairness in human interaction, that we too readily assume people generally understand. I've met, perhaps more than my share--being a lawyer--people who have no significant sensitivities in such matters. Surely, we can sharpen their sensitivities, we can help develop more appreciative understanding of what these values are, and I've even been prepared to try to sit down and draw up a list of this sort that really ought to be a part of what we concentrate on in the liberal arts curriculum. There's, of course, more to it. Relatedly, we really do run a serious risk of merely producing "products," people who when they go out in the world, indeed earlier than that, see that there are certain points where reason runs out. They are inclined, then, to conclude that anything goes. That worries me very much, and I think I see a fair amount of cynicism that is born of that.

Bruce Strasser: The rehabilitation of the word elitism is something desirable rather than something to deprecate. A rededication to learning and intellect is something which everyone should strive for, rather than the opposite, which is that everyone should be the same. So humanities courses, science courses, taken in common should be dedicated to achievement.

*From past comments, you all seem concerned with writing skills. Have you any specific proposals about that?

John Smith: Well, I'll say a word about that. It seems to me you attack this on two fronts. I entirely endorse what's been said about the importance of developing the ability to use the language with precision, to spell, not simply as kind of pedantic thing but so that people don't confuse the words. The spoonerisms and other malapropisms and so forth that come up in our student writing to the extent that where we're not sure, at least I'm often not sure, which word they do mean because of the way it's spelled. Now you attack that in two fronts. It

85

cannot be just the business of the English Department. You have to do it in every course where you have any written expression, where you intend people to put ideas together.

Then I think you also have to try to tackle it through some more high powered writing schemes. We have one, just beginning now, an Editors' Program. We've worked on it in the summer term. It's worked rather well. Because when you get a paper that comes out of method, it's a third draft and not a first, which means that a person has, at least in principle, two opportunities to look at the essay to see whether what they wrote is what they meant. Then I think we have to be somewhat more critical in the way of getting this material back to people in time for some sort of a second look. For many so-called term papers, the students never see them again until it's weeks and months later, and sometimes without a professor's comment. I think we have an obligation, if it's only spilling ink on the paper, to give the student some sense that we have read it, as distinct from what we sometimes do.

I think that it has to be shown that writing is hard, that clear thought is behind it. We have to get rid of people writing on "topics." I have a colleague who wrote a chapter in a book called Nature of Thought which is entitled, roughly, "Why you can't write a paper on George Washington." Well, George Washington is a topic: You have to start asking, "Was he a good statesman? Did he beat his wife?" That's to say, you've got to introduce some kind of a differential that an idea can be introduced and the mind begin to move around it, and see people wrestle with the attempt to answer a simple question in well-framed, relevant material and ultimately write what they mean to say. I find that people are remarkable at their ability to tell you what they meant to say if you bring them in afterwards. But there's often a very great gap for all of us between what actually is written and what we meant to say.

*Aren't some faculty simply overloaded with students? How can a person read 400 student essays? Who will fund this effort?

Robert Summers: Yes, that's very important. I'm more conscious of that then I normally am because at Cornell just now I'm going to be spending two weeks of the January break with six other people on the law faculty working on the first year legal writing program teaching 170 law students. That means my two week period for some research is gone. I mean, what you're putting your finger on is terribly important and you've got to get support from the administration. The teaching of writing is enormously time consuming. Now I'm no expert on the teaching of writing, of course, but I do have this one bit of experience. Over the years, in teaching writing to law students I found the single most important technique is this: You have them do the piece of writing. You go over it carefully, do a really critical job on it, and then ask them to re-do it in light of your criticism. Only if you do that, in my experience, can you really tell whether you got through to them. As Wittgenstein put it, the understanding is in the performance.

Now the other point I was going to make is this. One reason the writing thing comes up so often is that not only are students bad at expression; they're bad at thinking. The writing reveals it, dramatically. Often when I have lawyers tell me we don't do as good a job as we should in teaching our students how to write well, what the lawyers are really telling us is: You ought to do a better job teaching them how to think too, because the thinking itself, if poorly done, really shows itself on a piece of paper.

Richard Schmidt: The problem of dealing with people who control the budget and so forth is a very real one. I have great sympathy for any college president in the management of budget. We hear in the daily press that Johnny can't read, a criticism, particularly, of primary, secondary education in our country. We feel, also, tremendous concern over the amount of money being spent for education, as if the education should be directed toward the practical aspect, and the recitation of how you spell the word, with the great publicity about the national spelling bees. However, it's something we have to keep hammering at from every way that we can. The principles of using the basic tools of language, at least a native tongue, should have been learned before college. Maybe the elegance of expression, the polishing of style is a faculty job, but I'm afraid "basic" English is still undergraduate and even graduate school responsibility. I think I personally learned to write when I was a fellow after my doctorate.

*The implication of some of the discussion is that there is indeed a common experience every student should have. Isn't this, however, once again viewing the students as a product? I wouldn't bring this up, except that the architecture for schools, factories, and prisons has been nearly identical, beginning in the nineteenth century and continuing to the present. That itself tells us something about the educational enterprise.

John Smith: My main concern about the commodity way of thinking is that it seems to assume that I or you or any one of us, let's say, being scholars, worked in a field and we've mined some gems. We've gone into the dark places, the recesses, the forests at great risk to ourselves; we've mined these gems and we have them for sale to persons who are spared from going into those places. I am hired to dredge these things up and sell them for a price. Now that's just ridiculous because it isn't anything like that at all. The student and the teacher both face the same problems in the world and should aim to overcome ignorance and injustice. There it's a common attack with two individuals, I think, two stages of their development.

That's a very different model from the business where I am, so to speak, in between the student and the subject matter, shielding the student from the terrorists. We're both facing the terrorists; we're both facing ignorance and injustice at different stages of our lives and that's a subtle kind of dialogue, interplay, conversation. The notion of a product passing hands seems to me entirely inappropriate, because most of the time I am trying to elicit from the student an understanding of a point rather than merely delivering goods.

This is one of the reasons why we're still reading those Platonic Dialogues, and we're going to keep doing it even though it's very frustrating. The students read them and they say, "Where are the answers?" Well, the answers are to be figured out. There is no answer "there." The "answer" is in large measure what we go through as a search, as a process of discovery. Kierkegaard said a long time ago, that Socrates would be lost if the answers were in the back of the book!

Robert Summers: Well, what I have to add to that is the merest footnote. Many students that I have taught have something like the wood box theory of education. The head is the wood box. The professor's job is to fill it up with chunks of wood. There's a one to one transfer that takes place back and forth, but surely that deeply misconceives education. It's surely a process in which both participate. The liberal education of the undergraduate is surely a participatory process in which we seek to have an interaction and we hope that generates perspectives, understanding, skills, capabilities, sensitivities.

*What if colleges required a minimum of three term papers before graduation, as some European universities do?

Bruce Strasser: Writing is my business, and I'm not against that. However, I've found the only way to learn to write is like practicing the piano--you've got to do an awful lot of it. The way to do it is to do it every day. In fact if you don't do it every

89

day you'll dry up. And you have to do it under pressure. They have only an hour and they write off the top of their head. So, I would say, make people write something every night, even if it's only a page long. Eventually the juices will flow and they'll get better at it. The blocks will leave their mind psychologically so that they'll feel more comfortable in writing. In that sense, the type of course that you have in journalism is a very good way of getting people to improve their verbal ability, both orally and in writing.

John Smith: I entirely agree with that. I try to get students when they read not just to take those inane notes, page 28 "democracy," which when you go back to look at again you don't have any idea why you picked out page 28 and you even sometimes can't find the word "democracy" there. But try to get students to write a paragraph which expresses what the point was that they read. We all deceive ourselves if reading books turns out to be running one's eye over 135 lines every ten pages with comprehension. Stay for a moment. Write two paragraphs about what you took to be the basic point and even do it as a note to yourself. Page such and such, I think he's absolutely wrong here. He says this, and obviously the truth is this. This process would also help later writing, in any form.

*We're still dealing, in part, with generalizations. Could we be more specific about the common curriculum. What should it be and how should it be organized?

John Smith: Well, isn't it fairly obvious what it should be? Literature, science, philosophy, social science, history. I think we know what the general core would be. It's simply a matter of trying to get some advising system, short of just making it a matter of law, to get distribution over the subject areas. People are induced by argument, by gentle persuasion, by some regulations to give themselves a spread of these basic courses, so that when you get in the last couple years of an institution you have

90

some possibility of talking to a group of people who have some kind of a common background to which you can speak, so you can allude to common experience of imaginative literature, political science, philosophy, history. You can't do that if only one person in thirty or forty has read the material. But I don't know that one can really or should really make these generalizations which, by the way, don't bother me so much. The only way to be absolutely specific is to talk about what's going to happen in the next moment. But our colleges and institutions are so vastly different from one end of the country to the other that to speak too specifically is obviously going to be to speak falsely.

*Would the panelists think that a dual degree, such as engineering and liberal arts, would be valuable?

Bruce Strasser: I do know that at Bell Laboratories there's a premium put on that type of education--a dual degree. There's one thing they've got to come with. That's an expertise so they can make their payroll that week, that they're going to start producing something right away. So you've got to have expertise.

Moreover, the indication of the wider breadth of knowledge like the dual program will indicate that this person has capabilities far beyond just a narrow field of expertise. I think the industry is looking for capabilities in management.

*As this country is committed to mass higher education, isn't it particularly erroneous to insist that everyone has the same basic courses? There's too great a variety of abilities.

Richard Schmidt: Once again, I think that it's a mistake that we can have everyone come out with a common base of knowledge and a common base of experience. I also believe that we're going to have some who go through schools, colleges, universities, who might be considered exceptionally restricted people, yet make significant and great contributions to society. I speak of the brilliant grind who persists and even makes ethical discoveries. Some people in terms of communication eyeball to eyeball could be very good, but for other reasons would never be able to give a lecture, or write perfect prose. Yet they make contributions, even, at times, professionally. However, I think that one of the biggest difficulties which we're being asked to do is designing an undergraduate curriculum. I went through this experience in a way. I've assisted and chaired committees designing a professional curriculum, particularly, when it was popular to redesign and make radical changes, again during the 1960's, not as radical as were made in the liberal arts by the way. Some of these were exciting, some of them have fallen on hard times and go back to a more traditional approach. I think the hardest thing we have to do as said in the statement, "You now enter the company of educated men." How in the world do we do this? It was very clear how it was done in ages where authority was accepted and one could say, yet it consists of this and we translate this into two four-hour courses in English in the first year of college.

Robert Summers: One very fortunate thing is that we have this remarkable legacy. It is clear the answer to your questions, if there is one, would have had to be very very different not too many years ago. But isn't it the case that there are really very many very fine pieces of writing in philosophy, literature, history, that students of extremely different levels of preparation can find a great deal in. That is, if we give a classroom of students with great variety of background and preparation, one of these great pieces of writing such as by Plato, isn't there something in there for all of them? It seems to me, at least I just offer the suggestion, it seem to me that you take the route that I think is implied by the question: they may end up with no common experience. Yet in fact common materials provide scope for widely varying grasps. Indeed there'd be very great advantage. I can see very great advantage for having students inside the university, particularly in a small one, for the opportunity is really there, for having a common background of reading, of intellectual experience, even though it's true that a lot of students will take very different things away from it. Now this is somewhat like Hutchins. Surely there was something to what he said when he emphasized the values of having out in the universities ninety percent of the students going through a very common experience at about the same time. One very great thing about that is, of course, the obvious, that they'll <u>talk</u> to each other and they'll teach themselves and teach each other infinitely more than we can ever do. Now we lost that if we go this other route and say, oh, they're of such varying backgrounds and abilities that really we're in a straitjacket; we can't nurture their particular needs.

One reason why what you were saying sounds so appealing is that there's a great deal of misplaced liberalism in American education. There's a great deal of this notion that everybody should be free to do just about anything. Let them do their own thing, especially since they are of very differing abilities and backgrounds. Now it does seem to me that Hutchins had some powerful answers to all that, and I guess I put it tentatively. But I really think we've given up a great deal in abandoning the idea of the set book, for example. Oxford has set a book. Not that every student in the university does the same book, but within basic programs in the university, there are set books and the students talk to each other about them a great deal.

*But those students are the elite.

Well, but it's possible here. They're not that much the elite. I know Oxford pretty well. In the last 25 years there are big changes there, and students of greatly different backgrounds are admitted.

<u>Moderator</u>: We could debate for the next hundred years, as we have debated for the last

93

hundred, the specific courses that should be commonly required. I was struck by the fact that several times during the conference references were made to the loss of standards in the late 1960's and early 1970's. To put things in proper perspective I would cite a report to the Amherst faculty in 1945 which said that on most college campuses, remaining requirements for a B.A. depended on "something or other for a major." The same report also concluded that the "ability to write the English language," defined as passing a composition course, and "the ability to swim fifty yards," were required for a baccalaureate. So we have progressed beyond such statements, and should, and will continue to do so.

Contributors

John Edwin Smith, born in Brooklyn, New York, attended Columbia University and Union Theological Seminary. He is Clark Professor of Philosophy at Yale University. The author of several books, he has lectured at Harvard, Fordham, Princeton, Marquette and other universities. He has been chairman of the Yale philosophy department and director of the National Humanities Institute.

Robert S. Summers is McRoberts Professor of Law at Cornell University and is the author of a number of books and articles on legal subjects. A native of Oregon, Summers attended the University of Oregon, the University of Southhampton, England, as a Fulbright scholar, and Harvard University. He is the author of Law, Its Nature, Functions, and Limits, now in its third edition.

Richard P. Schmidt, M.D., was president of the SUNY Upstate Medical Center in Syracuse, was chairman for the National Committee for Research in Neurological and Communicative Disorders and of the Medical Advisory Board of the National Multiple Sclerosis Society. Currently he is Veterans Administration Distinguished Physician and Professor Emeritus of Neurology at the University of Florida.

A. Bartlett Giamatti has been a professor of Renaissance Literature. He was president of Yale University and is now President of the National Baseball League.

Bruce E. Strasser was executive director of information and publications at Bell Laboratories, where his responsibilities included public relations, publications, and public affairs for the company. Born in Rochester, New York, Bruce Strasser holds degrees from the school of engineering at Yale and from Columbia University, where he earned an M.A. in literature. He is now the head of his own firm of consulting, writing, and related disciplines.

Carey Brush holds a doctorate from Columbia University and is the author of a history of the state college at Oneonta, In Honor and Good Faith. He was academic vice-president at the same institution, serving as acting-president in 1987-1988.

Robert Moynihan, the editor of this volume, graduate from Regis College, Denver, Colorado, with a degree in history. He received an M.A. from the University of Colorado and the Ph.D. from the University of Arizona, Tucson. His A Recent Imagining, a work on the "Yale Critics," is published by Archon.

John E. Smith's "Three Dimensional Education" has been published in Education and Values, ed. Douglas Sloan, and appears here with the permission of Teachers College Press, Columbia University.

Bartlett Giamatti's "On Behalf of the Humanities" appears here with the permission of Atheneum Publishers, and imprint of Macmillan Publishing Company, which issued his The University and the Public Interest.